BMX RACING

BMX RACING

TOM JEFFRIES

WITH IAN THEWLIS

THE CROWOOD PRESS

First published in 2013 by
The Crowood Press Ltd
Ramsbury, Marlborough
Wiltshire SN8 2HR

www.crowood.com

British Library Cataloguing-in-Publication Data
A catalogue record for this book is available from the British Library.

ISBN 978 1 84797 454 9

Typeset by Jean Cussons Typesetting, Diss, Norfolk

Printed and bound in India by Replika Press

CONTENTS

ACKNOWLEDGEMENTS

To my parents for getting up at silly hours on their days off to take me racing for five years. Without their continued support this wouldn't have been possible, and I wouldn't be where I am now.

To the Bradford BMX Bandits, their Secretary Jeremy Brown and all of their riders for the use of their track and help with providing images for the book.

To Ian Thewlis for providing the 'Learning to Race' chapter.

To Johnathan Hearn at *Twenty24* magazine, Nikki Hawker and Roger Whilbraham for their help in getting me access to the Manchester indoor track for Round 3 of the National BMX Championships, and to Richard Robotham for showing me around the track.

To Martin Ogden and Identiti for the use of his bike and race kit for photographs.

CHAPTER I

WHAT IS BMX?

'BMX' stands for 'Bicycle Moto Cross', a reference to the way in which the sport first started. In the late 1960s, kids who could not afford motorbikes (but who still wanted to emulate their motocross heroes) started riding their bikes on tracks they had made themselves. From these humble beginnings BMX grew exponentially, gaining more and more popularity as a more affordable version of motocross.

Over the years, the establishment of sanctioning bodies pushed BMX forwards and gave it the status of an 'official' sport. The first governing body for BMX was formed in the early 1970s, and since then multiple official organizations have been set up across the world. This development ultimately allowed the sport of BMX to rise to the highest level of competition possible – The Olympic Games. BMX racing is now an officially recognized sport in over forty countries, many of which compete at both international and Olympic level.

Whilst there are many different forms of BMX (freestyle, trails, flatland, and so on), this book will concentrate on racing alone, as this

BMXers wait on a corner.

is the only form that is a recognized sport with well-established training methods and rules.

Readers of this book will have come to BMX via many different routes. They may have seen Olympic coverage, or footage on YouTube. They might have raced themselves 'back in the day' and be wondering what it is like now. Something will have got them interested. BMX is one of the most extreme forms of cycling, so what is it that drives people to go out into all weathers and ride a bike around a track?

For some it is the adrenaline. Pedalling as fast as possible at a jump, taking off and landing somewhere in the distance produces a big 'rush', and this is undeniably a significant

BMX IN FILMS

Joe Kid on a Sting-Ray is a film about BMX, following its development from the first races to its meteoric rise, and featuring interviews with riders from the past and present.

motivation for many of the people who ride. But the sport is not just for adrenaline junkies. Some people ride BMX for the sense of community. Whether they are elite riders training for Olympic Gold, or novices practising for fun, they all share a common interest and hobby. Whilst it is an individual sport

There is always more than one way to get across a jump.

BMX racing can be enjoyed by anyone of any age.

when the riders are out on the track in a race, outside of the racing they are all friends together. Racers help each other out at practice sessions – for example, offering new lines to take through straights – and there is generally a great atmosphere around the sport. The social side of BMX is a big part of its draw but the main reason people ride is just because it is fun.

There is nothing quite like the feeling of completing a goal through training hard. The goal may be a significant one, such as winning a first race, or something smaller, such as succeeding in setting off from the gate. Either

way, BMX is a very rewarding sport, and once you are hooked you will find it hard to stop.

BMX riding and racing are sports in which anyone can participate, regardless of age, gender, ability or finances. One of the best things about BMX is its accessibility and this is also one of the reasons why it has gained so much popularity. All it takes is a bike, a helmet, a track and some motivation.

Cycling is an excellent form of exercise and BMX not only works the legs, but also the arms, stomach and chest, whilst at the same time providing plenty of fresh air too. On average a person weighing 150 pounds

70kg) could burn around 550 calories doing BMX for an hour, making it a good way not just to lose weight, but to build muscle mass too.

BMX provides a great alternative sport for those who want something a bit different from the norm, and this is another key factor in its popularity. This book aims to give the reader a comprehensive introduction to the sport, giving advice on the equipment necessary, the tracks, the racing and some coaching techniques to help give everyone the confidence to start racing.

INJURIES?

BMX racers are made of tough stuff! Professional BMX racer Corben Sharrah broke his femur whilst competing at the World Championships on 30 July 2011. It could have been a career-ending injury but, after surgery and the insertion of titanium parts, he trained solidly and was back to riding on Supercross tracks just two months later, on 30 September 2011.

Supercross riders at the start of a race.

CHAPTER 2

SAFETY EQUIPMENT

BMX racing is an extreme sport, and as such there is a certain degree of risk associated with it. To minimize this risk, the rules indicate that some forms of safety equipment must be worn whilst riding. A number of further precautions can also be taken to reduce the chance of injury.

While all riders obviously hope never to fall off when riding, crashing is an inevitable part of BMX. It is important always to buy the best safety equipment you can afford as, in the event of a crash, it will be the only thing between you and the track. There is nothing worse than the feeling of not being able to ride your bike, and this is only exacerbated by injury. It is vitally important that you always wear the correct safety equipment at all times. It also helps to prevent any further, serious injuries that could occur in a crash.

A BMX club can dictate what safety equipment must be worn by its riders – usually a full-face helmet, gloves, long sleeves and long pants – but in reality every individual is responsible for their own personal safety and for the precautions they take. At the very least a helmet should be worn at all times. Not wearing a helmet while riding a bike is like not wearing a seatbelt while travelling in a car – potentially very dangerous. Even at low speeds, there is a far higher chance of injury if a rider is not wearing the necessary equipment.

Compulsory Safety Equipment

The rules relating to National racing state that certain items of equipment must be worn while riding on a BMX track. At the minimum, the following items are required.

Full-Face Helmet

There are several different types of helmet, including normal cycling ones, 'lid' or dirt-style helmets, and full-face helmets. Due to the dangerous nature of the sport of BMX, protecting your most important asset – your head – is vital. A full-face helmet covers almost all of the head, with just enough of a gap at the front for a good view ahead and for ventilation. Full-face helmets tend to be used in other extreme sports such as moto-cross and most disciplines of mountain biking; in the event of a crash, they provide much more protection for the rider than any other kind of helmet.

A CHAMPION'S EQUIPMENT

Gold medallist in the 2008 Olympics, Maris Strombergs: THE helmet and UFO shorts, and a ONE Bicycles frame.

A BMX racing helmet. Helmets are vital in BMX.

The main difference between a full-face and any other type of helmet is the chin-piece. This is because the helmet goes around the front of the face, which not only protects the chin more but also prevents the face from hitting the ground in a crash.

The outer shell of most BMX helmets is made from either ABS (acrylonitrile butadiene styrene), a kind of thermoplastic, or carbon fibre. The main advantage of a carbon-fibre helmet is that it is much lighter than an ABS helmet. This means that it puts less strain on the rider's neck while riding, making it more comfortable. However, it will be considerably more expensive than an ABS full-face helmet. The much more affordable ABS version will offer more than enough protection for BMX racing.

As well as the chin-piece, the helmet has a peak, to offer protection from the sun, and to prevent dirt, grit and water getting in to the rider's eyes.

While riding, it is imperative for a helmet to be strapped on properly. If it is not strapped on, there is no guarantee that it will stay on in a crash, and thus there would be no point in wearing it. There are two types of helmet strap: with a traditional 'D' lock and with a clip attachment. A 'D' lock has two 'D'-shaped rings on the strap on the left-hand side, and a long piece of fabric on the right-hand side. To fasten you put the long piece of fabric through both holes, then fold it around the second D, creating a loop, and put it back through the first one. This should create a tight lock, which can be adjusted to fit the head. The clip-in locks work in exactly the same way as the attachment on a car seatbelt. While this type of lock may be easier to use, it can be more temperamental, and in some extreme cases, the lock may break. Whilst this is unlikely for a novice, it is a point to be wary of when looking at helmets.

Gloves

Although they may seem much less important than a helmet when riding, gloves are required to protect the hands. Whilst riding a significant amount of strain is put through the rider's hands and into the grips, and this can cause blisters on the fingers and palms. Gloves act as a barrier between the hands and the grips and will also, in the event of a crash, protect the hands from scraping directly across the ground.

Only a full glove will do. Although fingerless gloves would help prevent blisters, they would be useless in a crash as they would leave the fingers unprotected from scraping along the ground, so they are not allowed.

BMX racing gloves are typically made out of light, breathable materials such as nylon and polyester. The material needs to be breathable to allow cooler air into the glove and warmer air out of it, thus preventing the rider's hands getting too hot. Both winter gloves and summer gloves are available – winter gloves have more padding and less breathability; summer gloves have less padding and more breathability – but realistically just one pair of gloves is enough.

Standard BMX racing gloves.

Jersey

The 2011 BMX rulebook states that a rider competing at National level must wear a jersey that has at least 3cm of excess material, and is not made of Lycra. However, while this type of jersey may be required at National level, the rule does not strictly apply to club events.

Rather than insisting on a specific jersey, clubs usually ask only that riders wear a top with long sleeves at their practice sessions,

A BMX jersey.

in order to protect the arms. Long sleeves offer effective protection against 'gravel rash', which can occur in the event of a crash, when an arm/leg/other body part is scraped against the ground, taking the skin off. A long-sleeved top may not protect against broken bones, but it should minimize the damage done to the rider in terms of superficial injuries.

Race Pants

Race pants are required when racing at National level and above; however, as is the case with jerseys, clubs are more than happy to let riders wear full-length trousers. Most riders wear an old pair of jeans.

Special race pants are made of tear-resistant, breathable materials, and generally have a leather patch on the inside of both knees. They are absolutely invaluable for the protection they offer, and will give a great deal more protection than jeans will against both contact with the ground and in the event of slipping a pedal. To increase the protection some, but not all, have removable padding around the hip and knee areas, to absorb more of the impact in a crash. However, they can be expensive, depending on the brand.

The vast majority of race pants available are designed for MX (motocross) racing. Whilst there are some companies that make pants specifically for BMX, there is really not much difference between the two. This is a positive, as pants that are designed to endure a crash from a motorbike are going to be more than suitable for crashes from a BMX bike, and so should last a long time.

Optional Safety Equipment

None of the mandatory items of equipment will offer anything more than limited protection against broken bones. They will offer some defence in the event of a crash, but not total safety. For those wanting more protection than is necessary, pad sets are available for almost every part of the body, to help prevent further injury in a big crash. Although such equipment is not required by the rule-

A rider with a Troy Lee Designs helmet.

book, and some riders will see no need for it (that is, until they are involved in a bad crash), many riders use at least one form of extra protection.

There are a number of reasons why some riders like to use extra safety equipment:

- **It adds confidence.** Wearing body armour or goggles can boost a rider's confidence more quickly than practising can. If a rider feels safer wearing protection that will absorb more of the force from a potential crash, he or she is more likely to try new things. Body armour adds a new, harder layer between the rider and the ground, causing the rider to be less afraid of crashing.
- **It is fashionable, or the top riders are doing it.** This is one of the main reasons why people wear extra protection such as goggles or a neck brace. As soon as the top riders introduce something new – a new technique, riding a certain way, or wearing a certain item of clothing – they are followed by other riders. One of the most recent examples is the wearing of golf gloves in an attempt to copy the pros.
- **They are well designed and look good.** Depending on the company that makes it, most of the safety items are interesting to look at, with extravagant designs, bright colours and striking lines. The appearance alone, especially of certain helmets, jerseys and pants, can make a rider want to buy and wear them.
- **It can put the rider in the right mindset.** If a rider wears his or her normal clothes while BMX racing, then there is nothing to differentiate between everyday life and racing. This is why some riders wear a race kit, as it prepares them mentally for riding, much as putting on overalls and helmet prepares a Formula One driver for a race.

BMX racing pants. These can help save a rider from scrapes and bruises to the legs.

Putting on race gear can help people 'get into the zone' – something that all athletes take very seriously.

- **It gives an air of authority.** On a track, the riders who are wearing a proper race kit look more experienced than those who are not. This can be enough for some riders, as it makes them look (and feel) like they know what they are doing. A British Cycling jersey might be enough to make you feel just the part, and benefit you by putting your fellow competitors into a negative mindset.

While some riders swear by the extra pieces of equipment, others choose not to wear it, for a number of different reasons:

15

Younger riders might benefit from wearing body armour to help increase their confidence.

- **It can be expensive to buy.** Inevitably, extra equipment costs extra money. Some riders choose not to wear items such as neck braces or body armour as these can be very costly, and at most levels are not needed.
- **It can restrict movement.** Some riders believe that wearing body armour or pads can prevent them being able to flow and move with the bike easily, which is a very important part of BMX. In reality it is not realistic and the technology is such that the safety equipment has evolved to be barely detectable when worn.
- **Style.** To some riders, how they look is as much a part of their riding as how they jump or manual, and they may see body armour as 'uncool'. Although this is not the case, it is a reason some people cite as to why they choose not to wear much protection.
- **Temperature.** Wearing an extra layer of clothing can make all the difference in cold weather. Similarly, wearing one layer extra in hot weather can cause much discomfort. Wearing the greater protection of body armour or pads can raise the body temperature significantly, but increasingly more breathable and vented materials are being used, and protection is constantly being improved to make it cooler whilst riding.
- **Extra weight and wind resistance.** Even though the effects may seem trivial, some riders use this as a reason not to wear extra protection. It seems unreasonable, however, since protection is getting lighter; the rider might be better looking at losing weight him or herself to counterbalance any potential weight gain that comes from the pads.

The equipment listed below is not required by the rulebook, but most riders use at least one of the items as it increases their safety and decreases their chance of injury. It is the rider's choice whether or not to wear any of the following items, and no one will be penalized for deciding to do so.

Goggles

Race goggles are worn by the majority of top

A rider wearing goggles.

riders in the sport. Made from plastic and with padding around the edges to increase comfort, they can be used in both wet and dry conditions. They fit in the gap in the helmet, covering the eyes and part of the cheeks. Goggles will keep water, gravel and dust out of the eyes, ensuring that the rider's vision is not affected by the elements, and will also protect the eyes in the event of a crash. Wearing goggles will certainly help to preserve one of the rider's most precious assets, both on and off the track: his or her eyesight.

Neck Brace

Neck braces are very new to the sport, and arrived around the time that Supercross tracks became more dangerous. They fit tightly around the neck and go down the back slightly to stop the head moving violently in a crash. While they are available for those who want them, they are both very expensive and unnecessary for beginners, who will not be reaching the same speeds as a professional BMX racer.

Body Armour

Some riders wear body armour underneath their jerseys to give them extra protection. There are many different brands offering many different levels of protection, but body armour (in its normal sense) is basically arm, back, shoulder and chest pads on one piece of clothing. Tight fitting, it usually consists of a breathable mesh top, with attached arm,

Neck braces come in all sizes for all ages.

Body armour includes a substantial back protector.

elbow, chest, shoulder and back pads to increase the protection. Seen as superfluous by many, it can give extra safety (and confidence) to those worried about injury.

Different companies have their own take on body armour, and designs differ slightly. For riders who are worried about it restricting movement, there is a t-shirt version and a vest version (which protects only the torso). These are suitable alternatives to the full version.

Body armour can be used to prevent gravel rash, as well as providing another barrier between rider and ground. Although it will not guarantee complete safety, it will offer

The front of the body armour shown above.

more protection against broken bones than a jersey alone.

Arm Pads

Arm pads (also known as elbow guards) are strapped around the forearm to protect that part of the limb as well as the elbow. They are made of plastic and are attached to a soft, breathable pad to add comfort. Made by many different companies, they come in a range of colours, materials and prices, and are worn underneath the jersey. They can also be used as an alternative to long sleeves and most clubs will be happy to let someone ride in a short-sleeved t-shirt if they have arm pads on.

Arm pads are mainly used to prevent gravel rash, although they may also offer some protection against more serious injuries such as broken bones or sprains.

Wrist Guards

BMX racers use their wrists a lot, and in the event of a crash it is only natural to put the arms out to try to break a fall. This has led to the advent of wrist guards. They may not be the most popular item of protective gear, but they can help to prevent broken wrists; this is because they are made from a breathable material with a stiff support bar built in, which limits the movement. This restriction in movement is what makes them unpopular but, as with most items of protective clothing, a rider who has had a crash while wearing them rarely rides again without!

Wrist guards are more commonly used by riders at the lower end of the sport, or by people who have broken or sprained a wrist in the past, and want to protect themselves as much as possible from further injury.

Race Shorts

It is becoming more commonplace to see riders wearing shorts and shin guards whilst racing BMX. This is because it can be more comfortable, as there is less material to restrict movement. Race shorts are also better ventilated and, therefore, cooler than race pants. Made from the same tear-resistant material as race pants, race shorts also have optional padding, to protect the hips.

Elbow guards can help cushion joints and stop further injury.

Knee protectors can be bulky, but are worth it.

The rulebook allows the wearing of race shorts at a National event, as long as they are worn with knee and shin pads. The shorts and knee pads combination is becoming increasingly popular across all skills of riders, from people just starting out all the way up to seasoned professionals.

Knee Pads

Knee pads typically cover both the knee and the shin, and are perhaps the most popular type of protective clothing after helmets and gloves. They are made out of a range of materials, most commonly plastic mounted on foam, to provide strength and comfort. Knee pads offer similar protection to arm pads, but on the lower limbs.

A rider's legs are one of the most important parts of his or her body for BMX racing, so protecting them from injury should be a main priority.

Knee pads will protect the legs from gravel rash, but they will also help prevent injury in the event of 'slipping a pedal'. This is when your foot slips off the pedal, and, as the weight shifts to the other foot, the opposite pedal is pushed down, which in turn spins the first pedal – most likely into your leg. This is very painful and can cause injury and leave scars, so knee or shin pads offer useful protection in this respect.

Knee or shin pads can be worn either with shorts, or on top of (or underneath) race pants.

Shoes

It may seem obvious, but wearing the correct shoe can significantly improve the safety of a BMX rider. Pumps are not suitable for BMX racing, as they are neither sturdy nor padded. Skateboarding-style shoes, on the other hand, are good, as they are padded on the inside, as well as being tough enough to put up with the stresses and strains of pedalling and crashing.

There are no real BMX racing-specific shoes; however, shoes that have been designed for use on or with mountain bikes are popular, as they are built to endure the same type of use.

Clipless shoes (see Chapter 3) are also acceptable in BMX racing, although at National events they are only allowed for those over thirteen years old. There is a 'clip' (or 'cleat') on the sole of the shoe, and this locks into a special 'clip' pedal. As the shoe is locked into (or clipped into) the pedal, this allows the rider to push one pedal down while simultaneously pulling the other pedal up, giving much more traction. The same principle is used on road bikes in races such as the Tour de France. BMX clips have to be more durable than road clips, as they are required to deal with the undulating stresses and strains of the BMX track, as well as being covered in more dirt and grit.

Clipless shoes and pedals are only for advanced riders or for those who have experience of riding with them, and should not be considered by a novice rider. While they can help a rider improve quickly, it is very difficult to unclip (take the shoe out of the pedal) in the event of a crash, which leads to an increased chance of injury.

Brands to Look Out For

There are many different manufacturers of protective gear, making many different types of protective clothing. This over-saturation of the safety-equipment market is further clouded by other types of cycling and motocross equipment, and this can really confuse people who are looking into buying protection for BMX riding. If in doubt, it is always worth asking at your local track or bike shop. Although there are not many purely BMX racing shops, MX and mountain-biking shops do stock many items that are suitable for BMX racing, so do not be afraid to go in and ask questions.

It is worth mentioning that all companies have different sizing standards. What may be a small in one brand may be a medium in another, so there is no substitute for trying gear on before buying. Again, ask at a shop, or ask around at your local club to see if anyone has any equipment for you to try on and get a feel for what might suit you.

There are hundreds of brands to choose from, but there are some companies that have consistently proven they can make high-quality products that are suitable for the BMX racing market.

Sixsixone (661)
Sixsixone make almost every form of protective gear available, from helmets and gloves

A rider in full race kit.

to body armour and shoes (although they do not make jerseys or race pants). They are one of the most prolific manufacturers of helmets, and there will always be at least one rider wearing 661 gloves at any track. They produce very well-made products with interesting designs at affordable prices. Most new riders wear something made by 661 as their products are cheap yet durable.

THE Industries
THE Industries make helmets, gloves, pads, shorts, jerseys, pants and a whole host of other BMX components such as seats and, most notably, number plates. Theirs is one of the most sought-after brands in BMX, and the company is famous for its exuberant and flamboyant designs. The products are of a very high quality, but they do come at a price. THE is the official (and only) number plate provider for the Supercross BMX races, and they also sponsor many of the riders who compete in BMX Supercross.

Fly
Fly racing make every kind of protective gear imaginable, and are another company known for making high-quality clothing in a range of outstanding designs and colours. Coming in slightly cheaper than THE but with the same build quality, Fly are a prolific manufacturer and riders always look good when wearing their clothes.

Fly have a proven track record with safety equipment used across the MX circuit, meaning that their products are very suitable for BMX.

Alpinestars
Alpinestars is a massive name in MX, although the brand is less well known in BMX. They make impeccable high-quality products for the MX market, which means that they are more than good enough for BMX, although

their prices do reflect the standard of their goods. For someone who is looking for amazing protection, Alpinestars will be a good bet.

Troy Lee Designs
A very well-known brand, Troy Lee Designs also make protection for MX riders. They are perhaps most famous for their helmets (due to their outlandish designs and irrefutable quality), although they also make pads, gloves and armour. Their products are more towards the top of the price range, but they will last a lifetime.

Oakley
Oakley is very famous in both MX and snowboarding, and is now establishing itself as a brand in BMX as well. They make top-quality gear for all price ranges, and are considered very fashionable in racing circles. Although they make t-shirts, gloves and other accessories, it is their goggles that have found most favour in BMX racing.

Bell
Bell makes good-quality helmets that are perhaps some of the cheapest available. Coming in a range of designs, Bell helmets have proven to be good enough in both BMX and mountain biking, so could be a good choice.

Giro
Giro is another company with a reputation for being cheap yet reliable. It makes gloves and helmets, as well as parts for almost any bike, whether for mountain biking, BMX or road cycling.

Shift
Shift make race kits for MX that are easily strong enough to use in BMX. Their jerseys, pants and gloves are relatively cheap and will suit riders of any age, height or ability.

CHAPTER 3

THE BMX BIKE

A BMX racing bike is different from the more common 'street' BMX bike that is usually found in bike shops. The most obvious difference is that it is much lighter. This is because a race bike does not need to stand up to the same pressures and strains whilst on the track as a BMX bike that is made for stunts. Race bikes need to be light – this will make them easier to manoeuvre, easier to control, and easier to jump.

Generally, race bikes also only have one brake – the back one. This is because grabbing the front brake at high speed could cause the rider to go over the handlebars, which is not a good thing. Front brakes can also be very fiddly to fit and, of course, would represent extra unnecessary weight.

The tyres on a racing BMX are much thinner than those on a standard bike. This gives much more responsive steering, allowing the

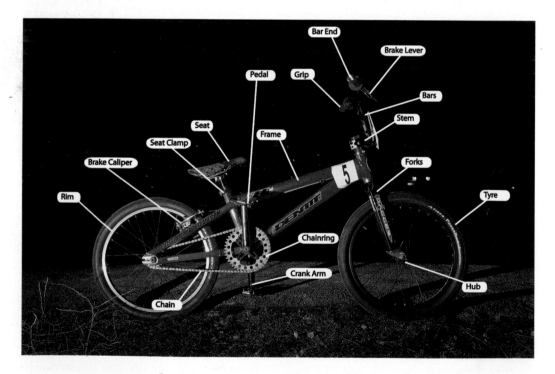

A labelled BMX bike.

rider to change direction quickly, to overtake or avoid other riders. They also come in a very wide variety of tread designs, with specific tyres for dry weather and wet weather. No prizes for guessing which is most likely on the UK tracks!

It is against the rules to race BMX with stunt pegs on, because it is very dangerous, and could cause serious injury to the rider, or to other riders. They need to be taken off any bike before it will be allowed on the track.

The main difference in the bike is the parts, which are all designed with racing specifically in mind. This means they are as light as possible, as reliable as they can be, and have been created with track riding in mind; making them very suitable for the job.

Bike terminology can be like a foreign language to some people, especially those new to the sport. The anatomy of a BMX racing bike is described below in a manner that should be easy to understand.

Frame

The frame is the main part of the bike, holding all the other elements of the bike together. Frames come in a plethora of different sizes, shapes, colours and makes, and choosing the right one is really just a matter of personal preference. There are several different measurements to look out for when buying a BMX bike:

- **Top tube.** This is the top part of the frame. A longer top tube will give the rider more room to move and make the bike more stable, whereas a shorter top tube will make it more reactive or 'twitchy'. Taller riders suit longer top tubes, and vice versa. The top-tube measurement is taken from where the frame meets the head tube at the front to where the frame meets the

seat tube in the middle. This is the measurement to look for when buying a BMX bike.
- **Chain stay.** The chain stay on a BMX bike is the length of the back end. This measurement is taken from the bottom bracket to the rear drop-out (the slot the back wheel goes in). A shorter chain stay is more responsive and easier to manual, whereas a longer chain stay is more stable and easier to ride.
- **Head-tube angle.** This angle reflects how steep the front of the bike is, and thus how fast it turns. Higher angles equal steeper forks and quicker turning, whereas lower angles mean more stability. 74 degrees is the BMX head-tube angle on a standard pro-sized frame.
- **Seat-tube angle.** The angle of the seat tube defines how the rider's centre of gravity will be placed. A steeper seat-tube angle will make the bike feel shorter, and move the rider's centre of gravity forwards. A slacker seat-tube angle will make the bike feel longer, moving the rider's centre of gravity closer to the back of the bike. However, it is worth remembering that, when riding a BMX, the rider will generally be standing on the pedals, so the position of the saddle, or the seat-tube angle, is much less relevant than it may be on a mountain bike.
- **Material.** The most common material for a race frame is aluminium, which is lightweight and strong. However, while it is not brittle, aluminium does 'fatigue'. This is the effect of the very slight bending of the frame being repeated time and again, causing small cracks. Because of this, an aluminium frame must always be considered as having a limited lifespan, of around 5 years, depending on use. Steel and its various alloys are also widely used. The most common of these materials is steel

chro-moly, an alloy of steel, chromium and molybdenum. At the top end of the market, carbon-fibre and titanium frames are available.

Bars

The bars (handlebars) are the part of the bike that the rider uses to determine which way he or she wants to turn, as well as being the part the rider holds on to. They come in a range of different rises (heights), widths, upsweeps (the angle upwards) and backsweeps (the angle towards the rider). Finding the right size is all a matter of personal preference, but generally a taller rider may suit taller bars, and vice versa.

Bar Ends

The bar ends are small round pieces of metal or plastic that go into either end of the handlebars. Whilst seemingly unnecessary, they are actually very important. If the rider lands on the handlebars in a crash, the bar ends will stop them from penetrating the skin, which would be both very painful and scarring. At only a couple of pounds for two, there is no excuse for not having bar ends.

Grips

The grips are the rubber bits on the handlebars that the rider holds on to when they ride, hence the name. They are available either in an ordinary version, or in a 'lock-on' version,

BMX bikes come in many different shapes and sizes.

which incorporates a plastic part underneath to reduce the chance of them slipping in the wet. Grips can cost as little as £5 and last a fairly long time, depending on how hard they are used.

Forks
The forks on a bike are the two 'legs' underneath the front of the frame, where the front wheel is located. They are made out of a range of materials for the lower-end bikes (steel, alloy, chro-moly), while the top-end race bikes typically use the more expensive carbon. This is because carbon is much lighter, making it easier to jump and manual the bike.

Stem
The stem holds the handlebars and forks on to the frame, making it a very important part of the bike. Stems only really have two variables: the material from which they are made and the reach. The material does not affect the ride at all, but it can affect the weight of the bike. The reach alters the steering of the bike by altering the effective head-tube angle. Generally, though, the rider's centre of gravity needs to be taken into account, too – taller riders normally benefit from having a longer reach, as this gives them more room for their body; a smaller reach will be more suitable for shorter riders, so the bars are not too far away from them.

Wheels and Tyres

Every bike has wheels (as does every car, every motorbike, and practically every mode of transport), so what makes BMX racing wheels so different? Well, the wheels on a race-ready BMX bike are usually very light, making sure there is no extra weight to slow the rider down. They are generally known as 20-inch wheels, and have 36 spokes going from the

Some riders like to colour-coordinate their kit and bike parts.

rim (the outer part of the wheel) into the hub (the inner part of the wheel). This balances the need for strength and weight perfectly. Wheels are very complicated when it comes to sizing, with two different sizes in use on '20-inch' wheels, so when looking into buying wheels, it is best to get advice from someone who knows what they are talking about.

There are many different types of tyre, all doing mainly the same thing. Made out of rubber, the tyres go around the inner tube (a smaller rubber ring that is pumped up to inflate the tyres) and help the bike to move forwards. Racing tyres come in a variety of sizes, treads (the pattern on the tyre) and brands, and picking the right one depends on a particular rider's riding style. Wider tyres will suit riders who want safety and stability, whereas riders who want responsiveness and speed will prefer a thinner tyre.

BMXers riding a Pro-sized frame typically go for tyres that are 1.75in wide on both the front and back wheels. However, riders who want extra stability might choose to run (use) 1.95in tyres, or even 2.10in tyres. Remember: the thinner the tyre, the less rolling resistance, and the less stability in corners.

Pedals

The pedals are the platforms on which the rider stands. There are two types of pedal: flat and clipless. Flats are used by riders of all skills, and they allow the rider to get on and off the bike easily, quickly and safely. They have pins sticking out of the flat part of the pedal, making it grip against the rider's shoes. The longer the pins, the grippier the pedal. Clip-less pedals (more commonly referred to as 'clips') are used by more experienced riders. They allow the rider to push one pedal down whilst pulling the other pedal up, giving them more power and speed. In order to use clip-less pedals a rider also needs clipless shoes, with a matching part on the sole, which is clipped into the pedal (see Chapter 2). Clips should only be used by very experienced (and confident) riders.

Cranks

The cranks (or crank arms) are the parts of the bike that connect the pedals to the chainring (see below). They come in two types: standard and spider. Standard cranks are just a single piece of metal with a hole at either end – one for the pedal and one for the axle (the part connecting the cranks). This means that they connect to the chainring in one place, which is just off-centre. Spider cranks have four or five 'legs' which come off the crank arm, hence the name. This means that connect to the

BIKE MAINTENANCE

As with all parts on your bike, it is important to ensure that the cranks are kept in good working order. If you tighten them up too much it will be harder to pedal, but if you fail to tighten them up enough you will suffer just as much. Making sure they are tightened correctly and well greased and maintained can help you to achieve your best results whilst racing.

chainring in more than one place. There is no difference in performance between the two; the only real reason for riding with a spider crank is to minimize the chance of bending the chainring. As it is connected in more than one place, the strain is spread across the chainring evenly. However, bending the chainring is not something that happens easily, and it need not concern a beginner.

Cranks come in many different lengths, which can be confusing. The 'standard' crank length is 175mm for a Pro-size bike, although other lengths are available. Longer crank arms are more suited to powerful riders or riders with long legs, whereas shorter cranks are more appropriate for riders who want to spin more, or who have shorter legs.

Chainring and Chain

The chainring (also called the sprocket) is the part that helps the bike to move forwards. This is because it is the part to which the chain is connected. When the rider pushes down on the pedal it moves the chainring, which then moves the chain, and that moves the freewheel (see below). This makes the back wheel turn, pushing the bike forwards.

Racing chainrings come in a number of different sizes, and have 'teeth' along the outside edge. The number of teeth determines how hard it is to pedal; the higher the number of teeth the harder it is to start pedalling, but then more speed is generated once the bike is in motion. With fewer teeth, it will be easier to start pedalling but the bike will start to spin (at which point it is not possible to generate any more speed) when it travels faster.

As with cranks, there are two types of chainring: standard and spider. The only difference is that the standard chainring has only one hole in the middle, for the axle to go through, and one slightly above it where the crank arm connects. Spider chainrings have no centre part, and four or five holes (depending on the crank arm) for it to connect to.

The chain's only job is to make sure that the chainring and the freewheel are connected. If they are not, then no matter how hard the rider pedals the bike will be going nowhere. There are a number of different chain types, however they all do (basically) the same job; a more expensive one will not necessarily be any more efficient.

For riders who are worried about bending/breaking their chain, heavy-duty BMX chains are available.

A BMX number plate. These are necessary for racing at any level.

Freewheel

The freewheel is part of the back wheel, and attaches to the rear hub. Pedalling moves the chain, which spins the freewheel, which, as it is attached to the back wheel, spins the wheel round. However, it only works one way, so that the bike does not stop dead when the rider stops pedalling.

The freewheel and the chainring are two of the most important parts of the bike, and should be cleaned, checked and maintained regularly. Like the chainring, the freewheel has teeth for the chain to fit over. These teeth are the only contact point between the chain and the freewheel, so it is vital to check regularly that they are clean and unbroken.

Brakes

Brake Lever

The brake is (or should be) one of the least-used parts on a bike. Race bikes only have a back brake. The brake lever is the part that is pulled to slow the bike down. Placed on either the left- or right-hand side (depending on personal preference), they are fairly cheap and, barring any major crashes, should last a fairly long time.

Riders most commonly have their brake lever on the right-hand side, but left-hand brake levers are available for those who are left-handed or who feel more comfortable having their right hand on the bars at all times.

Brake Cable

The brake cable is the wire that goes from the brake lever to the brake callipers. It is the only part that connects the brakes, and so should be checked regularly as prolonged use will stretch it, making it less effective. With regular maintenance they do last a very long time, if treated with care, and can be picked up for just a few pounds.

Brake Calliper

The brake calliper is the part that holds the brake pads (see *below*) in place, to make sure the bike actually stops when the brake is pulled. When the brake lever is pulled the callipers move inwards and push the brake pads against the wheel, making it, and the bike, slow down. When it is released, they move back out and stop the wheel from slowing down.

Brake Pads

The brake pads are the smallest visible part on the bike, and they simply squeeze against the wheel, causing friction, which slows it down. Racing brake pads are usually made out of rubber, as this makes for effective stopping power.

Seat, Seat Post and Clamp

The seat is where you sit down when you are having a rest from riding, or sitting at the gate. It is not used at all during the race, so it is very easy to save money on it, as seats can be picked up very cheaply. Because it does not need to be sturdy or durable, it is also possible to save weight on it, by buying the smallest available.

The seat post has only one job: to hold the seat in place. The seat post is another cheap part of the bike, and an easy component on which to save weight. It is a long piece of metal that fits inside the seat tube of the bike, and has a clamp at the top to hold the seat in place. Some people save on weight by cutting down the seat post and having just enough to keep it secure in the frame.

Some bar ends are made out of rubber.

The seat clamp is probably the cheapest part on the bike, with the sole job of keeping the seat in one place. It does this by holding a screw that is tightened around the frame and seat post so that it does not slip or move about when the bike is being ridden. It is attached to the top of the seat tube.

Size

As there are so many different sizes of bike, it can be quite confusing to know which one would be best for you or your child. If you are just starting out in BMX, or are thinking of upgrading your current bike, a complete bike will probably be the easiest option. Complete bikes come with all the necessary parts in the correct size and, although it may cost a little more in the short term, it is much quicker and easier to buy a complete bike than to build one. Building your own bike can be a rewarding challenge, but will cost more in the long term and take much more time. A happy medium between the two can be achieved by buying a complete bike and changing the parts on it as they wear out, or as you progress as a rider. This is the method most riders use for upgrading their bikes, and as long as you make sure that the new part matches the size of your bike, you will be good to go.

There are many different-sized bikes aimed at various sizes and ages of people. A four-year-old child obviously will not need the same size bike as a forty-year-old man. Whilst different riders will prefer different-sized bikes for various reasons, the following is a rough size guide:

- Micro Mini, for riders 3ft to 3ft 6in;
- Mini, for riders 3ft 2in to 4ft;
- Junior, for riders 4ft 3in to 4ft 10in;
- Expert, for riders 4ft 10in to 5ft 5in;
- Pro, for riders 5ft 6in to 5ft 8in;
- Pro XL, for riders 5ft 8in to 5ft 10in;
- Pro XXL, for riders 5ft 10in+.

This is a very rough size guide and there really is no substitute for just trying out a bike for size. However, as many bike shops do not carry race bikes, this can be a problem. Many clubs will have a range of bikes for loan or rent, or other members may allow you to try out their bike. In the meantime, do not be afraid of turning up at the club on your existing bike – chances are it will be more than suitable to get started with.

When looking at bike sizes, the badged size is not the be-all and end-all. Different manufacturers build bikes of different specifications, so one Junior bike may not be the same as another. For more on fitting a bike, see Chapter 7; for the time being, the following issues need to be considered:

- crank length is probably the most important consideration for sub-standard sizes (everything up to Pro);
- BMX frames should be sized lower than you would think;
- novice riders may prefer an oversize frame when first starting out as this will give more stability for the rider's size.

Brands to Look Out For

There are many different BMX bike brands out there for many different purposes. For example, a United BMX bike would be very good for stunts, but relatively useless on the track. To help you decide on a good bike for you, the following BMX racing brands are all well respected. It should be mentioned that most of these companies do make freestyle bikes as well, so be sure to buy one with the above sizing in the name. If you are unsure whether a particular bike is made for racing or tricks, be sure to ask.

Haro

Arguably one of the most famous brands in BMX racing, Haro Bikes have been around for over thirty years. They are known for amazing build quality and boundless rideability, so a Haro really would not be a bad choice of first bike. They come in a range of prices, typically very competitive.

Freeagent

Freeagent is another very famous brand in BMX, with a huge presence at National races in both the UK and the USA. The winner of the 2008 Elite Men's Olympic Gold medal Maris Strombergs is currently riding for Freeagent, as did the late Kyle Bennett (three-time World Champion). They were UCI BMX Team World Champions for four years in a row, which is testament to the quality of the bike.

Redline

Redline bikes are used by the entire Dutch National team, in a telling endorsement. They have had numerous wins in every possible category in the BMX circuit, and helped British rider Shanaze Reade to take the Elite Women's World title in 2007. Redline bikes can be quite expensive, especially as the 2012 Flight range has some bikes made almost entirely out of carbon fibre, however they will last a lifetime and will definitely help any rider win races. If you have your heart set on a Redline for your first bike, it is worth looking at buying a second-hand one.

Crupi

Crupi is a company that has been around (almost) since BMX first started. This has allowed them to constantly and consistently put out top-end parts and bikes that always look amazing and ride incredibly. Favoured by

many Elite riders, a Crupi is a famously good bike, but would most likely not be a good first purchase for a beginner as they can cost upwards of £1,000.

Intense

Intense is a company with a well-deserved reputation for producing a reliable, fast, responsive bike which suits most riders. The bikes are good all-round models, incredibly well built and versatile. Despite being relatively new to the BMX scene they have forged their reputation by producing bikes which can, and have, won races at all levels of competition. Clearly, there is a reason why so many Intense bikes are seen on the circuit.

GT

GT have been as much a part of BMX as any other brand. It is the brand of choice for 2011 Elite Men's World and European Champion Joris Daudet and 2008 Elite Men's Olympic Silver medallist Mike Day. With fair prices and such an immense track record, a GT could be a great first bike.

NEW TRACKS, OLD BIKES

'Old Skool' refers to the form of racing dedicated to old bikes. Riders (usually men who used to race on the old tracks and have rekindled their passion for racing) race on the modern tracks on bikes from the 1970s and 80s. Seen as both competitive and fun, Old Skool races take place at Regionals, and can sometimes have the highest number of entrants.

One

Relatively unknown, One makes top-end BMX bikes for experienced riders. Despite the lack of publicity in the UK, One (with Maris Strombergs riding) won the first ever Olympic Gold Medal for BMX racing, proving that they are a real force to be reckoned with.

Kuwahara

Kuwahara has been in BMX since the beginning. Perhaps most famous for their appearance in the film *E.T.*, they make well-priced bikes for all ages and abilities.

SE

One of the earliest bike manufacturers to come from BMX, SE Racing makes well-built bikes for every pocket. The 'retro' styling might not be to everyone's taste — it tends to be favoured by those who used to race in the early days and who want to get back into it.

Dialled

Dialled Bikes are a British company that sponsors riders in BMX, 4X and other cycling events. They make title-winning bikes with quality parts, and have a very good reputation in the UK.

A rider needs confidence in their bike to jump.

It should be mentioned that bikes from brands of BMX such as Mongoose, Huffy and Hoffman are not suitable for racing. While they may be more than suitable for park and street riding (doing stunts such as tailwhips and 360s), they have not been designed with racing in mind. This means they are relatively heavy, may have inappropriate parts (gyros, stunt pegs, and so on), and would not be right for learning to jump and manual on.

Buying Your First Bike

Once you are familiar with all the parts, sizes and brands to look out for, you will no doubt want to get out there and buy your first bike.

You may expect a Micro-sized BMX bike to be cheaper than a Pro-sized bike, as it requires fewer materials. However, in reality, costs for the smaller bikes are raised by lower manufacturing quantities and the require-ment for more specialist equipment. This can lead to a certain unpredictability in price for the various sizes and some bikes might seem to be surprisingly expensive, especially for a starter model. The best option is to go down to your local club and see if you can try differ-ent brands and sizes to make sure you buy the right one for you.

It is also a good idea to ask if anyone at the club is selling a bike, or knows of anyone who is. A second-hand bike will usually be cheaper than a brand-new one, which is always a good thing for those starting out. If you do buy second-hand, it is vital to check over the bike first. There are a number of things to look out for:

- **Tyres:** make sure the tyre has a decent amount of tread – 2–3mm is good enough – left on it. Bald tyres are not only slip-pery but also dangerous, and so should be avoided. That said it is very cheap and easy to replace them. Check to see if there are any splits or holes in the tyre, as buying a bike with a puncture already in it is going to be costly and annoying.
- **Brakes:** the brakes should work well and easily. If it takes 30m to stop at walking pace, there is probably something wrong. The brakes are a last resort so, if you pull them and nothing happens, it is probably not going to end well. Frequent checks and upkeep can help keep brakes in good working order.
- **Drivetrain:** the bottom bracket and free-wheel should run smoothly. If you can hear or feel grit or dirt in them, it will make the bike slower and harder to pedal. It is also tough to change these yourself, so making sure that the pedals, chainring and freewheel all rotate smoothly is the most important part of checking a bike over.
- **Frame:** there should be no cracks or obvious strains in the frame. Look closely at the welds on the frame, as these are the areas where cracks are most likely. Dents are also something to watch out for, although these are less serious. Cracks in the frame are unlikely as it will have had to go through some serious torture to happen; however, landing heavily on a cracked frame will only lead to one place: A&E.
- **Bars:** the bars are another place to watch out for cracks, as things will end up badly if they break mid-race. The bars must also be able to turn freely. It should be immediately obvious if there is dirt or grit in the headset, and this should be recti-fied by taking the stem off and cleaning thoroughly.
- **Forks:** the forks should be straight, undented and un-cracked; bent forks are more likely to snap or bend and this would not be beneficial when racing. Some forks

are designed with a bend already in them; on forks that have gone through a few crashes, the legs will not line up with each other.

- **Spokes:** the spokes should all be attached to the rim, tight, and not broken. This is simply checked by going round the wheels and making sure that all the spokes are as they should be. To check the tightness, pinch together two spokes lightly; if they move less than 1cm, they are good to go.
- **Chain:** the chain should be straight and all the links should be joined. If the chain is bent in any way then it is more likely to come off when pedalling hard. The same applies if any of the links are damaged. To make sure the chain is in proper working order, spin the cranks round slowly, inspecting each link from both sides. The chain tension should be checked too. A couple of centimetres play in the chain is fine, but a couple of inches could lead to disaster.

There are some general faults that can be found in a second-hand bike and, as ever, some are more likely than others. Because of the extreme treatment a BMX bike takes on a regular basis, its parts do need to be changed from time to time. Cracks in the frame, bars or forks are uncommon, and only ever result from a particularly bad crash. However, when buying an older bike that has seen extensive racing use, it is worth considering asking for an expert's opinion. A local club will usually have some experienced people who will happily advise you. The vast majority of people in the BMX community are friendly and helpful, and would never intentionally sell on a bad bike. If you find anything wrong with a bike during your inspection, you could either renegotiate the price or ask them to fix the problem for you. It is your money and your safety that you are looking after and if you are unsure, just ask somebody.

You should be able to pick up a good second-hand bike for around £200, or a brand-new one for around £300, depending on the brand and size.

Frequently Used Terms

There are a number of terms used in BMX to refer to specific parts of the bike, or groups of parts on the bike:

- **Gearing:** the amount of teeth on a chainring followed by the number of teeth on the freewheel. For example, with a 43t chainring (43-tooth) and a 15t freewheel, the gearing would be 43–15. This is a fairly typical gearing for a bike, although riders with more power might choose to ride a 44–16, while weaker riders could use a 42–15 to get up to full speed more quickly. The closer the numbers are, the 'spinnier' the gearing is.
- **Spinning:** this happens when a rider reaches the limit of how much he or she can pedal. When spinning, the rider is going so fast that pedalling does not make the bike go any faster, but simply spins the cranks.
- **Wheelset:** the wheels on the bike! For example, a Haro front wheel and a Haro back wheel would be a Haro wheelset.
- **Bearings:** there are two sets of bearings in a BMX bike – those in the headset and those in the bottom bracket.
- **Crankset:** in the same way that the wheels are called the wheelset, the cranks together are called the crankset.
- **Steerer tube:** the long part at the top of the forks. Because the forks have to connect to the rest of the bike safely, there

is a top part that goes through the frame, through the stem, and connects through the bike by the steerer bolt.

- **Steerer bolt:** also known as the 'top cap', the bolt goes in the top of the steerer tube. It has a screw in the top which is tightened to pull the forks and the stem together, making the forks tighter against the frame.
- **Cut/uncut:** some riders cut down elements of their bike, to make them fit the size they want. The three main parts that are cut down are the seat post (to save on weight – if the extra 10cm of metal in the frame are not being used, there is no point in having them); the bars (a rider with a narrower arm span might cut down their bars to make them shorter end to end); and the forks' steerer tube (if the steerer tube comes too far out the top of the frame, it may be cut down to make it fit).

- **Spacers:** rings of plastic that come in specific sizes, usually 1in or 1cm. They go around the steerer tube of the forks, and can be placed underneath or on top of the stem. This can make the bars feel higher or lower, depending on how they are placed. If you feel you are leaning over the front of the bike too much, putting spacers underneath the stem can be a cheap and effective way to fix this.
- **Chain tensioners:** fixed on the axle of the rear wheel on both sides, these parts act

Riders on smaller-sized bikes.

to stop the back wheel slipping, by 'butting up' against the rear drop-outs. There are little adjustable pins on either side which are moved so that they are pushing against the frame. These, along with the nuts on the rear wheel, stop it from moving about too much.

- **Headset:** a ring of ball-bearings that goes in the top-front part of the frame, where the fork's steerer tube comes through.

Frequently Asked Questions

Why is the bike so light?

Saving weight on a BMX bike is important because the lighter it is, the easier it is to manoeuvre in the air, in the berms and on the track. An agile BMX bike is necessary so you can make split-second overtakes to win the race. It is also easier to jump a light bike, so the least weight possible is a priority for most riders. BMX racing is not 'freestyle'. Freestyle, by definition, is about trying new things, which can frequently go wrong, so the bike needs to be strong enough to withstand potential disasters. BMX racing is very much a fixed style, so the most experienced racers can get away with using very light materials because they know exactly what the bike will need to do.

Why are some bikes longer than others?

In BMX racing there are two types of bike: 20in BMX bikes and 24in Cruisers. Cruisers have 24in wheels, and this makes them more stable and easier to predict than a 20in BMX. Cruisers are normally used by riders who are either older or less willing to crash, as the increased solidity of the bike makes it more predictable.

Should the brake lever be on the left- or the right-hand side?

While most riders have it on the right, it is simply a matter of personal preference. A left-handed rider may prefer to have the brake on the left, and a right-hander may like to have it on the right. Often, BMX riders will own and ride another bike, and will opt to put the brake on their BMX on the same side as the main brake on their other bike. On a road bike, the main brake will be the back brake, probably on the right; on a mountain bike it is more likely to be on the left.

What is the right material for my bike's frame?

There are two answers to this question. The first relates to weight. Some materials weigh less than others and, as the frame is the heaviest part of the bike, this is one place where weight may be saved. The second answer is that some materials 'flex' (bend slightly) more than others. A steel frame will be much stiffer than an aluminium one, and some racers prefer this stiffness as it makes the frame feel more rigid. Again, this is down to personal preference and the chances are that someone just starting out in BMX will not notice the difference between the two.

Which gearing should I go for?

As with most of the questions, it is up to the rider. 43–15 is a good place to start, as this is a very common gearing in BMX and it is easy to go up or down from there.

CHAPTER 4

THE BMX TRACK

BMX tracks come in a plethora of different shapes, sizes, layouts and materials, but they all have the same basic components: a gate, some jumps and a finish line. That is basically all a BMX track is: start, jumps, finish. The order is always the same (after all, it is not possible to finish before starting), but there are two main ways in which tracks differ: size and jump layout.

There are many different types of jumps (and even more jump variations), so there are an infinite number of possible track layouts. They also differ in terms of size because some tracks have bigger jumps than other tracks. For example, one track's biggest jump might be 20ft, whereas another track's biggest jump could be 30ft. The height of the jump usually correlates to its length, so that a 30ft jump

A BMX track in use.

might have a take-off that is 6ft high, to help the riders jump it more easily.

The Start

At the start of a BMX track is the start hill, which is exactly what it sounds like: a hill where the riders start. The size of the start hill usually reflects how big the track will be. A tall and/or steep start hill will lead to a big track with big jumps, whereas a track with smaller jumps will have a lower and/or flatter start hill. Pedalling down the start hill launches the rider at the track, enabling him or her to increase speed at the start of the race.

Also at the start of every single BMX track is a gate, which is made up of two parts: a ramp and the actual 'gate'. The ramp is at the same angle as the start hill, and has eight lanes. Lane 1 is (most commonly) the inside lane, while Lane 8 is the outside lane. It's at the same angle as the track to help the riders to balance against the gate. It is usually made out of metal (with rough ridges to help the tyres grip), or sometimes concrete, the same material as the start hill. It is around one and a half bike lengths long, so the riders have enough room for their bike, and also enough room to roll back from the start gate.

The gate itself is a long metal bar, 1–2ft (30–60cm) off the ground, which moves down ('drops') at the start of the race. When not in use, it stays in the 'dropped' position, flush with the ramp and the track. It also has rough ridges on, and placing the tyre in between these ridges helps rider and bike to stay upright when sitting on the gate. When the gate is in use, its movement is controlled by a ram and a controller box. The ram is fixed to the gate and to the ramp part. When the start button is pressed on the controller box there will be five beeps, to signal that the gate is about to lift and should not be ridden

over. The ram then lifts the gate to the 'up' position, at which point the riders will get on to the gate. Pressing another button starts the cadence, the voice and beeps that act as a warning before the gate drops. 'All right riders, random start. Riders ready, watch the gate' will sound, followed after a random time period of 0–8 seconds by another five beeps, each one correlating to a light on the traffic light, plus an extra one for once the gate has dropped. On the fourth beep (and green light), the ram will push the gate down, allowing the riders to ride the track.

There are two types of BMX gate: a standard gate and a safety gate. A standard gate has a single piece of metal that goes from one side of the gate to the other. It has no protection between the gate and the 'drop zone' (where the gate drops to). It is the most common gate in BMX, with almost every track having one of this type.

The safety gate is similar to a normal gate, but it has a metal barrel running from the top of the gate to the drop zone. This prevents riders from injury, should they go over the gate. Although this type of gate is preferable to the standard version, they are very expensive, and most clubs are unable to afford them. They are most likely to be found at tracks in which a significant amount of money has been invested.

Visible from the gate are two sets of traffic lights (or just one, depending on the track). BMX lights look similar to the traffic lights used on the road, but they have two ambers, rather than one. When the race is about to begin and the start sequence has begun, the lights will be off. As the random countdown ends and the cadence (beeps) begins, there will be five beeps – one for every light, and the additional one for once the gate has dropped. The gate drops on the green light, and the race begins. For more on this, see Chapter 5.

After the start hill some tracks will have a speed bump, also known as a roller. This single bump in the ground, normally about 12in (30cm) high, is the first obstacle to overcome. They are not found on all tracks, but they are becoming more and more popular. They are designed to slow the racers down slightly, and give them less time to prepare for the first jump. Rollers can be placed anywhere on the track, but the most common place to find one is at the bottom of the start hill.

Jumps

After the initial parts of the track, it then (typically) levels out, and the jumps begin. There are two parts to the jump: the take-off and the landing. The take-off is the part where the riders literally 'take off'. This is the first section of the jump, which is where the ground starts to rise, helping to lift the riders over the jump. The size of the take-off depends on the size of the jump – the longer the jump the bigger the take-off is likely to be, and vice versa. The landing is where the rider lands, and typically looks the same as the take-off. Big jumps are likely to have big landings, as this will help riders control the bike when they land.

There are many, many different variations of jump, but there are a number of main types.

Tabletop

A tabletop jump is perhaps the easiest kind of jump to manoeuvre, and this is because it is flat. A tabletop is made up of a take-off, a flat section, and a landing. It is called a 'tabletop' because the middle, flat section looks like the top of a table. Tabletops can be placed anywhere on a track, and can be any size.

For riders wanting to find their first jump to try, a tabletop is the best and safest option. This is because its flat top section allows riders to come up short ('rim' the jump) and have a far smaller chance of falling off.

Double

Perhaps the most iconic jump in BMX racing, the double is also the most prevalent. A double is essentially made up of two raised rollers. The 'double' refers to the fact that it has two 'lips', or areas where the jump rises then falls. The two rollers are connected by the middle part. This is usually rounded, making the jump look like a portion of a circle on the inside, however, some are flat in the middle. Almost every track has at least one double.

A tabletop jump.

A double jump, with two 'lips' at the take-off and landing.

Riders looking to start manualling should begin with a double, as the smooth centre portion teaches good technique, helping the rider to get the front wheel up and over the second lip and at the same time ensuring that they do so in a smooth motion.

Triple

A triple is very similar to a double, as it is basically a double with an extra lip in the middle. Triples are usually bigger than doubles and can be the hardest jump through which to maintain speed. Although they are not as common as doubles, most tracks have a triple at some point.

Riders learning to double manual should start on this type of jump, as the two sections help riders to learn the correct technique.

Step-Up

A step-up is a combination of a tabletop and a double, with the flat middle part of a tabletop and the lip on the landing of a double. It is called a step-up because the landing of the jump is higher than the take-off. Step-ups are very common in BMX, and most tracks have one (or a variation of one).

To get over step-ups easily the rider can lift the front wheel onto the initial table part of the jump, then lift the front wheel over the lip at the landing of the jump, or manual it or jump it. Jumping should only be attempted by experienced riders, as there is an increased chance of crashing, due to the change in elevation. For more on techniques on how to traverse jumps effectively, see Chapter 7.

Step-Down

A step-down is a step-up jump that has been turned around 180 degrees. The lip is at the take-off but not the landing, making the

A triple jump.

A step-up jump, so called because the landing starts higher than the take-off.

landing lower than the take-off. This explains the 'down' part of the name, as it makes the rider go down. The step-down is far less commonly found than any other main type of jump.

Step-downs are relatively safe, due to the lower landing, however, they should still be treated with care.

Rhythm Section

A rhythm section is usually placed at the end of the track, and can take up the entire final straight. Rhythm sections are designed so that the riders cannot pedal, and have to use their pumping, jumping and manualling skills to get through them. There are no set rules for what a rhythm straight can and cannot contain, but there are three main types. The first one involves constant rollers. This is where a series of closely spaced rollers all join together to form one constant straight. The second type comprises small jumps, all set closely together. This could be, for example, a 4ft step-up followed by a 4ft double followed by a 5ft tabletop, and ending in two small doubles. The final type is a combination of the first two. While any of the above types of rhythm straight may be found (or, indeed, none at all, as some tracks do not have them), the latter is most likely.

Rhythm sections are a great place for a rider to work on his or her skills, as the jumps

A rhythm section.

Not all rhythm sections are the same; different tracks have different set-ups.

are much smaller than those on the rest of the track, and they encourage consistency and rhythm. Children and newer riders can learn any kind of skill on a rhythm section.

Variations on Jumps

Although the above jumps are the main types found on BMX tracks, some jumps are variations on existing jumps. For example, a double could have a landing that is higher than the take-off; it will still be a double, but in this case it will be known as a step-up double. Similarly, a triple on which the rider lands further down than the take-off would be called a step-down triple. As long as you know the main types of jump, you will be able to identify the variations that are found at different tracks.

One type of jump that is becoming more popular in BMX currently is the step-up step-down. This jump has a step-up merged with a step-down, with the two lips creating a double in between them. These types of jumps offer many possibilities in terms of the routes through them, making them more of a challenge.

Berms

A berm is the name given to a corner. Berms are normally 180-degree banked turns linking two straights, but some will be less than 180 degrees, depending on the track layout. Usually in a half bowl shape (a bowl cut down the middle), berms are where the riders all

A BMX track.

ABOVE: *A dog-leg berm. Not all berms are U-shaped.*

Some berms are 'unbalanced', and may have shorter runs into or out of them.

come close together, and where many races are won and lost. It is very easy to make mistakes in the berms while racing, as it is not always possible to take the same line through a berm in a race as would be taken in practice.

There are two different types of berm, distinguished by the type of material from which they are made. Some berms are made out of the same material as the rest of the track. This makes for more fun racing, but they are very hard to maintain and are easily affected by the rain and other adverse weather conditions. Alternatively, berms may be made out of tarmac. This type is becoming more commonplace, with almost every track opting for it, since tarmac is a much harder compound and the berms require relatively little upkeep.

Pro Section

Some, but not all, tracks have what is known as a 'pro section'. This is where a track has two different straights, both going the same way, and both starting and ending in the same berms, but with one straight – the pro section – having much bigger jumps than the other. The pro section will be quicker to go through (if the rider jumps everything), but it will be much tougher to ride. This means that, if it is ridden correctly, a pro section can be used by a rider to overtake riders who have opted for the easier side.

Although not all tracks have pro sections, they are becoming more widespread among British tracks, and are gaining popularity for their emphasis on tactics and skill.

Finish Line

At the end of the track is the finish line, where the track, and the race, end. Riders must make

sure that they keep pedalling right up until the finish line. It is extremely frustrating to be overtaken by another rider on the line just because of failing to put in the extra two pedals.

What Makes a Good BMX Track?

There are no real hard and fast rules as to what makes a good BMX track. Some people may prefer tarmac berms, whereas others prefer dirt berms. Some tracks suit those who can manual better; others suit riders who are particularly good at jumping. Personal preference and riding style play a big part in the appeal of certain tracks, but there are a number of key points that most people use in order to judge the quality of a BMX track:

If the track has been well kept and maintained, it is generally seen as a 'good' track. There are certain points to look out for:

- The condition of the track should be good, with no divots or ruts in the take-off or landing of jumps.
- The ground should be firm (even after rain).
- There should be nothing protruding (rocks, stones, wires) from the jumps.
- The track itself should be grass-free (although the sides of the jumps may have some grass).
- The berms should not be waterlogged or rutted.
- Take-offs and landings should be even, and without bulges.
- The track should not have too much loose gravel.
- The gate should be solid, with no broken pieces of metal.

Most people consider a track to be good if it caters to a wide range of skills and ages

ABOVE: A standard BMX gate.   *BELOW: Riders snapping out of the gate.*

A BMX start hill.

— for example, if a five-year-old can get the same amount of enjoyment out of a track as a thirty-year-old professional.

These are standard concerns that any club should keep in mind when they meet at the track to make sure that it is safe enough to ride. It is very unlikely that a track that has regular club sessions will fall foul of any of these points, and even tracks with no regular club sessions will rarely be totally unrideable.

It is easy to spot the difference between a good track and a bad track — at the highest level of competition in Supercross or Olympic racing, for example, it is clear to see how well the tracks are maintained. It is also possible to 'feel' the condition of a track while riding it.

OPPOSITE: *Riders lining up to the gate.*

Track Layout

BMX tracks have several different kinds of layouts, in terms of both jumps and circulation. All BMX tracks have different jumps in a different order, and they may also have different layouts geographically.

Some tracks are built so that the riders go downhill and such tracks typically follow an 'S' shape. Riders go down the first straight, turn 180 degrees, go down the second straight, which is facing the opposite direction to the first, and so on until the finish line. However not all tracks are downhill, and not all tracks follow the 'S'-shaped layout. Some tracks have a first straight, followed by a very long first berm (which goes around the third and fourth straights), making the last two straights inside the first two. Other tracks do not follow this at all, and have a completely different layout. It is up to the track designer and the club which way the track is laid out.

49

A speed bump. These are used as an extra obstacle for riders to overcome before a jump.

BMX tracks do not have to have four straights. Some tracks have more straights, and some have fewer. Again, this is the choice of the track designer and club.

Different Types of Track

There are many different kinds of BMX tracks, which all differ in terms of size, shape, layout and quality.

Pump Track

Pump tracks are very small tracks that have very small jumps. They are simply rhythm sections in the shape of a track, joined together by small berms. Pump tracks are designed to help riders improve their pumping by not allowing any room for pedalling.

They make riders work harder to gain and maintain their speed through them, teaching them how to pump effectively. They are the smallest type of track – some people have even built them in their back garden – and also the cheapest to build.

Play Track

Play tracks are bigger than pump tracks, but just smaller than full-sized BMX tracks. They have smaller jumps, smaller start hills, and typically are not as long as a standard BMX track. They are designed for fun, and to teach skills such as jumping and manualling on a smaller jump, which can then be transferred on to the normal-size BMX track.

BMX Track

A BMX track is usually around 400m long, from

start to finish. This is the most prevalent kind of track, made up of all of the usual components, and the place where most people start. There are varying levels of BMX track, and these all depend on the quality. There is the standard BMX track, the Regional standard track (tracks capable of holding Regional races), National standard tracks (tracks capable of holding National races), European standard tracks (tracks capable of holding European races) and International standard tracks (tracks capable of holding races such as the World Championships). Most tracks in the UK are of either Regional standard or National standard.

Riders on a rhythm section

A rhythm section from a rider's point of view.

Supercross Track

This is a completely new breed of track, designed for Supercross racing, which is an even more extreme version of BMX racing; see Chapter 6. Supercross tracks have an 8m start hill, with jumps of over 35 feet. It takes some serious time and dedication to even be able to think about riding one of these tracks. They are the type seen in Supercross races and the Olympics.

Best Tracks in the UK

The UK has an impressive array of very high-standard BMX tracks, which produce some very high-standard riders. Personal preferences may vary, but the following tracks are those that are generally held in the highest regard.

Platt Fields, Manchester

One of the tracks used by the British Cycling Talent Team, the outdoor track in Manchester is another track that has a very good reputation. With good facilities and good standards, despite being relatively new the track has already hosted multiple National rounds, and has been the training ground for future Olympic hopefuls.

Manchester Indoor Track, National Cycling Centre

One of the newest tracks in the UK, the indoor Supercross track was finished in 2011. Costing a total of £24 million, the indoor BMX track in the National Cycling Centre (NCC) is one of a tiny number of Supercross tracks in the UK today. In the heart of the NCC (where the Velodrome is also located), this track has some of the best facilities imaginable and is definitely one of the best. The fact that it is indoors means that it is protected from the elements, which can only help to preserve its quality. Like the Platt Fields track, it is also home to many Olympic hopefuls.

Tipkinder Park BMX Track, Crewe

Built by the renowned Clark and Kent Contractors (or C&K as they are also known), the Crewe BMX track is known for its steep, fast, downhill layout. With dirt berms and a big pro-section jump, Crewe has proven to be a favourite with everyone, from young children to seasoned pros, and the fans. Crewe also holds the Bob Fields Grands, a race held in memory of the former coach of Olympic BMX rider Shanaze Reade.

Kent Cyclopark

Another C&K venture, the Cyclopark in Kent has tracks for almost all types of cycling, making it a very good facility. It held the Southern Championships in 2011 and opened to the public in 2012.

Facilities

Due to variations in funding and location, BMX tracks in the UK have differing levels of facilities available to them. While the following facilities may not be integral to the running of a club, most BMX racing clubs would hope to have some or all of them.

- **Storage container:** most BMX tracks run by a club will have a standard shipping container next to them, which is used for the storage of bikes, safety equipment, parts necessary to run their practice and race sessions (such as the traffic lights) and other BMX paraphernalia. It also gives them a place to run the sessions from that is protected from the weather.
- **Designated parking:** some tracks (although not all) have tarmacked car-parking areas, but this is simply not an option for some.

A U-shaped berm.

Tracks that are in, and run by, a park (such as the track at Hartlepool) are most likely to have parking areas.

- **Floodlights:** these are relatively new to BMX racing, but are becoming more and more popular. They allow practice sessions to be held in the evenings, even in winter, where previously they could only be held at weekends outside of the summer season.

- **Fencing:** some tracks have a fence around the perimeter, making them more secure and more aesthetically pleasing. Fences ensure that only the correct type of bike

Not all tracks look the same or have the same layout.

TOP: *Containers are good to use during club sessions, but can be prone to abuse by graffiti artists.*

BELOW: *A BMX track illuminated by floodlights.*

gets on to a BMX track, and prevent motorbikes from being brought on.

- **Toilets:** it must be said that toilets are not a common commodity at most BMX tracks, although tracks in parks are more likely to have them. Some clubs do rent temporary facilities for Regional races, while for National races, which take place over two days, there are more likely to be some sort of facilities for riders and spectators to use.

- **Seating:** spectator seating is not commonly seen at tracks, with the exception of the indoor track at Manchester. While it may not be necessary for practice sessions, it can be advisable to bring a chair to long race days.

- **Food:** it is up to each club whether they choose to sell food at their meetings. Most clubs will sell something at their practice sessions and club races, from snacks right up to hot meals. As the

55

A rider jumping, with seating behind him.

competition level rises and more riders come to the track, more food is generally available. There is usually a burger van at races at Regional level and upwards, although it is sensible not to rely on this at an event.

- **Podium:** some tracks have a dedicated podium for prizegiving, while others have a makeshift one.

BMX tracks all differ in the way they are set out and built, and in terms of the level of facilities they offer. No two tracks are alike, and this means that it is always best to have a well-rounded skillset when riding, rather than spending a lot of time on just one aspect of the sport.

Riders waiting on a berm.

CHAPTER 5

THE BMX RACE AND STARTING RACING

Once you have your safety equipment and your bike, you know all about the various parts of the track, and you feel confident enough, it is time to race.

Racing is the end to which all of the training, hard work and sacrifice go. It lets you see how well you can ride next to your competitors, and it gives you results that you can then use to improve your riding. It is what every rider — young, old, skilled and novice — looks forward to, and every rider on race day will be feeling the same mix of excitement, nerves and anticipation.

Whatever your reason for considering BMX racing, you have made the right decision.

It is a fast-paced, exciting extreme sport that demands both physical and mental fitness, and it could be argued that it offers a mixture of adrenaline and action that is unparalleled in any other Olympic sport. It is also one of the easiest sports to start — as long as you can ride a bike, you can ride BMX.

BMX IN THE UK

There are over forty BMX racing clubs in the UK, including two in Scotland and one on the Isle of Man.

BMX races do not stop for the rain.

Race Day

If you are new to the sport and it is your first race, you will need to familiarize yourself with things like where to race, the pre-race procedure, and the race itself.

Registration

At any race event, all riders have to register to ride. Registration usually takes place in or around the container (or whatever serves as the club 'office') at club races, while at National or higher level races it may be elsewhere. Registration is very simple: the rider's name, race number and date of birth are required so that the rider can be allocated to the correct category. There may also be a legal notice to sign, making sure that every rider takes responsibility for his or her own safety, and will not attempt to sue in case of accident or injury.

Categories

There are many different categories across the various different competition levels; however, the chances are that your first race will be a club race. Club races are divided up into seven separate categories, based on age and skill. A rider will be placed in a category based on age first, but if they perform well in a race (finish in the top two or three, for example) they can be moved up a formula to make the racing more challenging for them and fairer for the rest of the category. This also works the other way, so if a rider finishes in the bottom two or three in a category (and if they are young enough), they will be moved down a formula to race with riders of similar skill.

There are seven race categories used at club races:

- **They Really Ought to Have More Sense (TROHMS):** the category for riders who are over 'a certain age', and are perhaps not the most skilled riders at the track. The racing is typically slower, so this category is a good place to start BMX racing for riders aged 16+. Some, if not most, riders will be on the more controllable Cruiser-style BMX bike in this category.
- **Formula 5:** the class for the youngest children, regularly featuring riders aged four to six, depending on skill level. This class will usually offer some sort of award for its riders – a medal or trophy – to motivate them to come back and continue riding.
- **Formula 4:** aimed at riders aged six to nine, who are slightly more experienced at racing. It offers more of a challenge for younger riders than Formula 5 does, but it is not overly difficult.
- **Formula 3:** the class for ten- to thirteen-year-olds, and the intermediate level group. Racing is quicker than in the lower classes, and there is more of a difference between Formula 3 and 4 than there is between Formula 4 and 5.
- **Formula 2:** aimed at riders who are aged eleven to fourteen, with more skills than those in Formula 3. The racing is fast, and riders in this category are usually looking at moving up into Formula 1.
- **Formula 1:** aimed at riders who are aged thirteen plus, and are slightly less skilled than those in Superclass. The racing is fast and competitive.
- **Superclass:** the fastest category, in which only the best and fastest riders are able to race. Riders can race in this class from age fifteen plus. Superclass requires the highest amount of skill, so only the very best riders in the club will race in it, sometimes for money prizes.

There is leeway between the different formulas or categories; for example, a rider aged eight would be allowed to race in Formula 3 if he or she was far more skilled than others of his or her age. Similarly, a rider aged fourteen could race in Formula 3 if he or she was new to the sport, or under-skilled, however this is not actively encouraged. Due to the size differences between children, riding in classes which are drastically out of their age or skill range is not advised as it can be dangerous. Transferring between categories will have to be sanctioned by an official. Ultimately, the club will know its riders and their skill level, and will assign people to the appropriate categories.

Although it is used regularly at club races, Formula racing is not restricted to club races, and can also be run else-where. Classes can be merged if there are not enough riders in two separate categories. For example, if a Formula 3 race has two riders and the Formula 2 has three, the two groupings will be merged into a race with five people. The points would still be allocated in the same way – the racer finishing first in Formula 3 but fourth in the race would receive full points for winning their category.

Moto Sheets

Each race is called a 'moto' (basically a 'heat'). There are usually three motos, followed by a final. The motos determine who will progress in which order. For example, a category with fourteen riders in it would have two gates of seven riders, splitting them evenly. These two gates of riders would then race their three motos, with riders receiving points relating to where they finish. First place gets one point, second gets two, third place gets three, and so on. After the three motos have been raced, the official adds up all the individual riders'

MOTO	FIRST	SECOND	THIRD
They Really Ought to Have More Sense (8 Gate Motos)			
Please Check your race Number carefully			
422	MOTO 1 - GATE 3	MOTO 8 - GATE 8	
181	MOTO 1 - GATE 1	MOTO 8 - GATE 6	
66	MOTO 1 - GATE 7	MOTO 8 - GATE 4	
MTB	MOTO 1 - GATE 5	MOTO 8 - GATE 2	
49	MOTO 1 - GATE 2	MOTO 8 - GATE 5	
1.4	MOTO 1 - GATE 4	MOTO 8 - GATE 7	
P11	MOTO 1 - GATE 6	MOTO 8 - GATE 1	
FORMULA 5 (8 Gate Motos)			
Please Check your race Number carefully			
3.4	MOTO 2 - GATE 3	MOTO 9 - GATE 8	
07	MOTO 2 - GATE 7	MOTO 9 - GATE 4	
46	MOTO 2 - GATE 4	MOTO 9 - GATE 7	
45	MOTO 2 - GATE 5	MOTO 9 - GATE 2	
B1.2	MOTO 2 - GATE 6	MOTO 9 - GATE 1	
23	MOTO 2 - GATE 2	MOTO 9 - GATE 5	
918	MOTO 2 - GATE 1	MOTO 9 - GATE 6	
FORMULA 4 (8 Gate Motos)			
Please Check your race Number carefully			
J9	MOTO 3 - GATE 5	MOTO 10 - GATE 2	
J2	MOTO 3 - GATE 2	MOTO 10 - GATE 5	
2.4	MOTO 3 - GATE 6	MOTO 10 - GATE 1	
30	MOTO 3 - GATE 1	MOTO 10 - GATE 6	
25	MOTO 3 - GATE 3	MOTO 10 - GATE 8	
26	MOTO 3 - GATE 4	MOTO 10 - GATE 7	
FORMULA 3 (8 Gate Motos)			
Please Check your race Number carefully			
4.4	MOTO 4 - GATE 2	MOTO 11 - GATE 5	
09	MOTO 4 - GATE 4	MOTO 11 - GATE 7	
1001	MOTO 4 - GATE 6	MOTO 11 - GATE 1	
045	MOTO 4 - GATE 1	MOTO 11 - GATE 6	
8.4	MOTO 4 - GATE 3	MOTO 11 - GATE 8	
243	MOTO 4 - GATE 5	MOTO 11 - GATE 2	
FORMULA 2 (8 Gate Motos)			
Please Check your race Number carefully			
32	MOTO 5 - GATE 2	MOTO 12 - GATE 5	
35	MOTO 5 - GATE 1	MOTO 12 - GATE 6	
617	MOTO 5 - GATE 3	MOTO 12 - GATE 8	

A standard moto sheet.

Riders waiting for the gate to drop.

points, and the eight riders with the lowest number of points overall are put into the A final. The riders with more points get put into a B final. In the event that two or more riders have the same number of points, a semi-final will be run to determine who progresses.

The moto sheets tell the riders which category they are in, the number of their race, the gate number they have for each moto, and who they will be racing.

The Pens

The pens are where the riders wait for their race. Some clubs have dedicated areas for this with metal railings to make sure each rider is in the correct area, whereas other clubs either use makeshift ones out of tape or have none at all. It is usually very obvious where to wait at club races (just follow everyone else), but races at Regional level upwards can be very strict. A race day will run more smoothly

if all the riders are in the correct waiting area and, when there are over 100 races in a day, this is essential.

The Start

The BMX Gate

There are two parts to the BMX gate (see page 39) – the ramp and the gate itself. The gate has eight lanes numbered one to eight, with lane one (normally) being the inside lane, and lane eight being the outside lane. The lanes can also be referred to as 'gates'. At a BMX race or practice session, the riders line up behind their gate, and wait for the race before them to start. Once the preceding riders have been released, the starter (the person controlling the gate) will raise the gate, with five beeps being heard before it rises. Once it is in the upright position the riders

Riders waiting on the gate.

can get on to the gate and start to balance in preparation for their own race.

Traffic Lights and the Cadence

The traffic lights look very similar to traffic lights on the road, except that BMX racing lights have a red light at the top, followed by two amber lights, and then green. The reason for this is the extra light gives the riders more time to 'snap' (see Chapter 7) and thus get a better start.

Before the gate is dropped, the starter will shout 'Attention', to signal that the race is about to start. He or she will then start the 'cadence', which is the start sequence for the race. Whilst there are several different types of starts, the one used in the UK is called a 'random start', and this means that there is a

The BMX traffic lights.

random amount of time between the start of the cadence and the gate dropping. Once the button has been pressed, there will be a warning of 'OK riders, random start. Riders ready, watch the gate', and a pause of 0–8 seconds before the lights come on and the gate drops. The lights come on individually, and the gate drops on the green. There will also be five beeps (one at the same time as each light and the gate dropping) to help with the start. This all happens very quickly, and good reaction times are key to getting a good start in a BMX race.

The Race Itself

Once the gate has dropped, the race begins and all eight riders will be battling it out for the top spot. It is vital to remember that the race does not finish until the first rider crosses the line.

Races usually last around forty seconds at the higher end of the sport, although this obviously increases or decreases in relation to the length of the track.

While racing, riders can roll, pick-up, manual or jump any obstacle they want to in order to

> **'HOLESHOT'**
>
> The 'holeshot' is the term used in BMX to refer to the person who reaches the first corner first. When commentators say that 'X or Y has the holeshot', they simply mean that X or Y is in first.

Crashes in BMX are common.

BMX racers jumping.

get the best position possible – there are no rules regarding what can or cannot be done over a jump. It is usually easiest to stick to what has worked best for you in practice, but this may not always be possible. For example, if you were to get overtaken aggressively in a berm, you might not have enough speed to manual a certain jump, or to jump the next double. This is why it is a good idea in practice to try getting through jumps in as many different ways as possible, in order to be prepared in case something does not go to plan in a race.

As well as having a 'back-up plan' for how to get over jumps, you should also try your 'racing line' in practice sessions. This is because you will not be taking the same line through a berm in a race as you would in practice – you will turn much shallower in a race than at a gate session – and it is important to know

Jumping can be the quickest way to get over a jump.

Riders and parents checking the moto sheets.

whether you will have enough speed to get over jumps in a race.

Just as it is sensible to try your racing line through berms in practice, it is also worth doing full laps before a race. It is a waste of time to spend a couple of hours perfecting the last straight, only to discover in the race that you are too tired to do anything other than roll the last two straights. This sort of practice will also help to build stamina, which is a staple of BMX racing, as any racer will tell you.

BMX racing is considered a non-contact sport, but contact between riders on the track during a race can happen – indeed, with eight riders all trying to get the same spot on the track, it is more or less inevitable – so all riders need to be wary of either colliding with someone else or being ridden into themselves. The berms in particular are the most common part of the track for this to happen, as it is the place where all the riders come together and fight for position. Sticking to your line and keeping an eye on what is happening around you is the best way to avoid being taken out by a competitor.

Finally, remember to keep pedalling right until the finish line. Titles can be won and lost on the final jump, and it is frustrating to lose a race just for the sake of putting in one or two extra pedals.

Where to Race

Club Racing

There are no rules as to where to go for a first race, or what level it should be, but it is advisable to go to a local track for a club race if you have not raced before. The fees will be lower, the distance travelled will be shorter, and there will be less competition. Club races have the lowest amount of riders as it is usually only the riders of the club who are racing, unlike Nationals where riders from all over the country will turn up to race. This lower level of skill and competitiveness will help a novice to learn the basics of BMX racing, and get more of a taste of what it is like to race.

Most clubs have a website detailing when their practice sessions and races are, so look online and do not be afraid to just turn up at a meeting. There is no fee for watching, and this may be just the encouragement you need to give racing a go yourself.

Joining a Club

When you start BMX racing, joining a club can be beneficial for many reasons:

- **Lower fees:** clubs charge a membership fee, and then club members pay lower fees for gates and for racing, to motivate people to join the club. More members means more money for the club and more helpers and organizers.
- **Community:** while it is only you out there on the track in a race, everyone in a club works together to help each other ride. Having a fully accredited BMX club behind you will definitely help you enjoy and compete in BMX racing.
- **Club-only events:** clubs will often run events (training sessions, meetings, advice, and so on) exclusively for members and being a member of a club means that you will constantly be kept up to date with what is going on.

Club clothing: jerseys, hoodies, number plates, and so on, with the club name or logo printed on them are often used to promote the club. These are (sometimes) cheaper than kit in the shops, so they not only help to identify the club to which you belong, but may also save you money.

Setting up a Bike for a Race

When going to your first race, it is important to check that your bike is race-ready. Ensuring that there are no worrying cracks or unexplained noises can help you get the best performance from both you and your bike. As well as the checks covered in Chapter 3 ('Buying Your First Bike'), there are a number of further steps you can take to prevent all of your training going to waste.

Any abnormal noises coming from your bike can cause not only poor performance from the bike itself, but also poor performance from you. Confidence plays a major part in BMX racing, and making sure your bike is running as well as possible can help

Riders riding down the start hill.

Two riders after a crash. Checking your bike carefully after a crash is vital.

BELOW: Manualling can help you get to the front of the race.

The berm can be a good place to overtake.

to increase that confidence before a race. A niggling worry can cause havoc with your mental agility, and can even be more detrimental to your race than the fault itself. You do not want to be worrying when you get on the gate, so, if in doubt, get it checked out.

A thorough check of your bike is always advisable before and after a race, and the main points to look at are the following:

Headset: make sure the headset runs smoothly, without any noticeable grinding or tight spots. This will help you to make quicker and easier turns, enabling you to make crucial overtakes or avoid obstacles on the track. If it needs cleaning, take the stem off the forks, slide the steerer tube out of the frame, and take the headset out. Take the ball-bearing ring out of the frame and re-grease it, before placing it back in the frame and putting the bike back together. This should be done regularly, but especially before racing.

Grips: if you have 'normal' grips (not lock-on grips), check to see if there is any movement by simply twisting them round, as if trying to take them off or rev a motorbike. If they move more than a few millimetres, they could benefit from being dried out. To do this, take the grips off (using compressed air can help with this), dry off both the handlebar and the inside of the grip, then spray hairspray, deodorant or compressed air into the grip to help it stick to the handlebar.

Wheels: the wheels must be free-running. While there is not much you can do to prepare the wheels before a race other than cleaning them, you can clean the teeth of the freewheel so that the chain can run more smoothly. This will help you to accelerate and pedal more quickly, helping

ABOVE: A rider checks behind during a race.

Riders tackling a speed bump in a race.

Supercross riders jumping.

Younger riders exiting a berm in a race.

you to go faster. To clean the teeth of the freewheel, simply use a cloth to remove any dirt or grime from the contact points.

Brake: it is important to make sure that the brake works before any riding, but especially before races. Nobody knows what might happen in a race, and if you need to pull your brake halfway through a lap, you want to know that it is going to work. To check the brake, either adjust the brake callipers (making sure they are as tight as possible to the wheel when used) or unscrew the section of the brake lever where the cable goes in. The further out the parts are, the tighter the brake will be, and vice versa.

Chainring: as with the freewheel, cleaning the chainring before a race can help to increase traction by making it easier for the chain to fit over the teeth. The chain coming off during a race is both painful and preventable, so making sure that everything works as it should do will help you get the best result possible.

Chain: make sure the chain is straight, with no missing or broken links. While there is not much you can do to a broken chain other than replacing it (which may not be possible just before a race), you can always oil or grease the chain, making it more flexible and thus easier to pedal. Ensuring that any moving parts on your bike are suitably oiled (you can use WD40 for this) can help to make sure you reach your potential in a race. Another important thing to check with the chain is tension. If the chain is not tight enough, it will be more likely to come off, and will also not provide as much power. Around an inch of movement (tested by pushing the chain up and down) is suitable for racing. To tighten the chain, simply loosen the back wheel and move it backwards until the tension is correct. (To loosen the chain, move the back wheel forwards.) Then adjust the chain tensioners accordingly and tighten the back wheel up again.

Overtaking in corners happens quite frequently.

Spokes: check the spokes before a race to make sure they are tight and unbroken. There is not much to be done about a broken spoke just before a race (other than avoiding putting too much strain into that particular wheel during a race); fortunately, a single broken spoke will not overly hamper your race. Repairing broken spokes is a difficult task, and not one that should be tackled by anyone who does not have proper training. To check the tension of the spokes, take two spokes that are next to each other and pinch them together slightly. If they move more than a centimetre, they should be tightened with a special 'spoke key', which fits over the nipple part of the spoke. This needs to be done both regularly and carefully; if you do

ABOVE: *Looking where you are going is vital to winning.*

RIGHT: *The inside line is shorter than the outside line.*

Tyres: there should be a good amount of grip on the tyres. A minimum of 2–3mm of tread is acceptable for practice, but in a race around 5–6mm would be safer. While some riders change their tyres depending on the track and track conditions (a tyre with more grip for a wet track, or a tyre with less rolling resistance for a smooth, dry track, for example), this is both an advanced and expensive technique, and is not something a novice will need to worry about.

Two Cruiser riders racing.

Getting to the first corner in front of the pack allows you to control the race.

not have the tool or the expertise to do it, ask someone who does.

As always, it is a good idea to seek the help of a local bike shop or bike mechanic if there is any uncertainty.

What to Wear at Your First Race

When competing at your first race there are no set rules as to what you can and cannot wear, other than those regarding protection (see Chapter 2). There are certain pieces of

protection that are required in BMX racing. You should always wear a helmet, gloves and clothing that fully covers your arms and legs while riding to make sure you are suitably prepared for a crash. Extra protection may also be worn, but this is optional.

It is advisable to wear old clothing, because BMX tracks are made from dirt and gravel, and can become very dirty when wet. Clothes often get covered in mud when racing, or torn in the event of a fall, so they should be comfortable and not too special, until (or if) you decide to purchase specific racing gear.

The club running the track may also be selling race jerseys and hoodies with its name

Supercross racing is fierce, with riders reaching up to 40mph (65km/h).

Riders of all ages compete in BMX racing.

and logo on. This not only helps to raise the profile of the club at higher-class events such as Nationals, but also gives club members a sense of unity.

Before thinking about your first race, you need to have put in adequate time on the track to make sure you are comfortable both with your riding and in your equipment. Race situations are very different from practice sessions, and you may feel more exposed while racing than when riding in an everyday session. As a general rule of thumb, wear the equipment that you would wear while riding normally, then add further equipment should you feel it to be necessary. Even though many riders do not use the added protection of body armour or wrist guards, it is down to the individual to make that decision. It is your body, so you can wear as much extra protection as you feel necessary.

A rider receives a medal after winning.

CHAPTER 6

COMPETITION STRUCTURE

Throughout the UK, Europe and the world, there are many different types and levels of competition. Ranging from the easiest (novice racing) to the highest level possible (Super-cross), these competitions are entered by people of all ages at all stages of their BMX careers. There is a race for everyone, from the experienced veteran to the newest and youngest riders.

The competition structure in BMX resembles an upside-down triangle. At the bottom is club racing, with a small number of riders and easy racing, progressing on into Regionals, with more riders and harder racing, rising to the World Championships, with a huge number of riders and an unparalleled amount of skill required. At the top is the Olympics. To compete at this level, riders need to prove themselves through a rigorous selection process before they will even be considered. On the other hand, the Worlds can be entered by (almost) anyone who wants to race.

Although BMX racing really is an international sport, the following covers the structure in the UK only.

Levels of Competition

The different levels of competition have been created for different skills and ages, ensuring a fun experience for all. They are as follows:

Novice Racing

Novice races are designed to be entered by people who are new to BMX, and who have very little experience of racing. The pace is slow, and very little is done in the way of jumping/manualling, but every rider tries their hardest and it is a great place to start.

Novice races are typically held only at Regionals, however club races do have classes that are capable of handling novice riders. As novice races are held at Regionals they tend to have the same amount of photographic coverage as Regional races, with perhaps less emphasis on where the riders finish, as no points are awarded.

A track used by novice riders should be able to host a Regional, which means that it will have the same level of facilities and track maintenance as might be expected at a Regional-level track. This means suitable parking, decent upkeep and most likely a storage container, although this is not necessary.

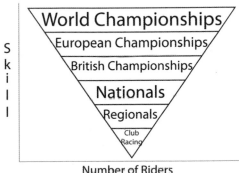

The BMX racing hierarchy.

To race BMX at novice to Regional level, every rider needs to have a number plate attached to the handlebars of the bike, to identify him or her to the commentator. It also helps the people on the finish line allocate the correct points to every rider. According to the policies of British Cycling (as set out in the Rulebook that can be found online at british-cycling.org.uk/), at National level upwards, the number needs to have either

… A) Their previous year's National ranking number, B) A current World Championship number prefixed 'W' in the class it was awarded in or its nearest equivalent, C) A current European Championship number prefixed 'E' in the class it was awarded in or its nearest equivalent, D) A current British Championship '01' number in the class it was awarded in or its nearest equivalent, or E) The last three digits of the rider's British Cycling Licence number.

This must also be accompanied by a side plate placed over the top of the frame, which should have the same number on either side.

Novice races are not as popular as 'expert' level races (see Regionals), and usually have fewer competitors – more than two full gates of novice riders in one category is rare. This is because a rider will see a faster improvement in his or her riding as a result of taking part in a class that is at a slightly higher level than their own, rather than one that they can win easily. For more on this, see Chapter 7.

Club Racing

Club races are run by a club, at its own track. Although they are open to anybody, they are usually entered by the members of the club. As a result of this, the difficulty will vary from race to race and club to club, as each will have

WHO'S IN CHARGE?

British Cycling governs not only BMX racing, but also almost all cycling events in the UK, including cyclo-cross, mountain biking, road and track riding (to name a few).

Riders lining up on the berm.

Focusing on the traffic lights is important for getting a good gate start.

different abilities of rider. Club races are run in a 'formula' style, with riders being placed into a formula based on age and ability, making the racing fair but challenging. There is no differentiation between genders – there are rarely enough girls of similar ages at club events to constitute an entire class.

Club races are held across seasons – most commonly summer and winter – and there are points available at every race. These points accumulate over the season and the rider with the most points at the end of the series gets the title. Club races are held at practically every track in the UK that has a club based at it, making them incredibly easy to find and enter.

Almost all riders in the UK will compete at club races at their respective clubs across the country. The numbers of riders at club races will vary greatly, but some races may attract as many as seventy competitors.

There is relatively little coverage of club races, mainly because they only concern the club and its riders. Some clubs may have a rider or volunteer who writes any race reports for them, or perhaps someone who acts as a photographer.

Club racing is the cheapest of all forms of BMX racing, with entry fees of around £3 per race.

Regionals

The UK is divided into seven regions: the North (northregionbmx.co.uk), the Midlands (midlandsregionalbmx.co.uk), East Anglia (bmxeast.com), Scotland, the Isle of Man, the South (southbmx.co.uk) and the South-West. Each region holds around eight races, or one for each club within that region. Regionals are classified on age and gender, with single, 'expert' age groups (five to six, six to seven, and so on) up to the age of sixteen, from

A sponsored rider.

which point riders can choose to race either sixteen to twenty-nine or Payback. Sixteen to twenty-nine follows the same trend in skill as the other age categories, whereas Payback is aimed at the faster riders who are looking for more of a challenge. The races are the same as the other categories; however, as well as points, cash is awarded to the two fastest riders at the end of each event. This makes the class highly competitive, attracting only the best riders in the region.

Unlike club races, Regionals operate a 'best of' points system: out of all eight races, the best six results are taken and added together to generate a final total. This places less emphasis on going to every race in order to get more points, and it also allows for the occasional bad finish or crash. This is used at all levels equal to or higher than Regional races.

Points are allocated in the same way in all categories:

Overall position	Points
1st in the A final	50
2nd in the A final	47
3rd in the A final	45
4th in the A final	44
5th in the A final	43
6th in the A final	42
1st in the B final	35
2nd in the B final	32
3rd in the B final	30

Almost all tracks in the UK will be of at least Regional standard, with very few failing to meet the requirements. Things such as parking, track upkeep and facilities all play their part in bringing a track up to standard, and any track that regularly hosts a club meeting will almost certainly be of Regional level.

In order to race at Regional level and above in the UK, riders are required to have a British Cycling (BC) membership and race licence. British Cycling is the governing body for all cycling events within the UK, and sets rules, requirements and provisos for the practice of BMX racing. The membership and licence are both annual costs, and have to be renewed every year.

Regional races attract anywhere up to 160 riders, with participants coming from across their respective regions and clubs.

Regional races can expect slightly more coverage than a club race, with one or more photographers attending. Individual clubs may also do a report on how their riders did at the event, but there is not usually an 'overall' report on the day.

Racing at Regional level is more expensive than club racing, costing £5 for a novice class, £8 to race in an expert class (age category)

and £10 to race in Payback. Of course, there are the race licence and membership costs to add on to this, as well as variable amounts in petrol to think about (the North region, for example, covers any club from Hartlepool to Crewe).

To find out which region you are in, either consult someone at your club or look at the British Cycling website. It is worth mentioning that, while most regions operate in more or less the same manner, some may have slightly different ways of running their events. This can affect the number of races in a season (more races will be harder to organize), the number of volunteers they have or the number of riders the races commonly attract.

Nationals

National races are held over a weekend, and consist of two days' racing. They work in the same way as Regionals – motos, quarter-finals, semi-finals, finals – but they attract a far greater number of riders, with people from all

Riders at Nationals need to have correctly coloured number plates.

over the UK coming to race. National races can involve as many as 900 riders, which is why single rounds are held over an entire day. They are held all around the country. As an example, the 2012 UK BMX National series took place between January and August, at Manchester (rounds one to three), Birmingham (rounds four and five), Braintree (rounds six and seven), Derby (rounds eight and nine) and Peterborough (rounds ten and eleven).

National categories are the same as Regional categories – individual age groups up to seventeen years – but with dedicated Cruiser classes as well.

National races have slightly different rules to club, novice and Regional races, because of the higher competition level. For a start, riders in National races are required to wear clothing with at least '3 cm doubled-up excess material, without stretching the fabric. This shall be measured by pinching the fabric between the index finger and thumb' (quote from 'Rule no. 6.1.056 – Jersey', found on the website of the Union Cycliste Internationale, uci.ch).

While racing at Nationals, all riders must ensure that they have the correct number-plate colours. It is not a problem at Regional races, but British Cycling rules state that, as they follow the same rules as International level races, riders must stick to the following guidelines, 'with the exception of current British Champions and World/European finalists who may choose to use their Championship plates and numbers'. The colours used in the 2012 season were as follows:

- **Elite Men:** white plate, black numbers;
- **Junior Men:** black plate, white numbers;
- **Championship Women:** black plate, white numbers;
- **Men/Boys:** yellow plate, white numbers;

The fastest way to get through a jump might not always be jumping.

Supercross races attract riders from around the world.

- **Girls:** blue plate, white numbers;
- **Cruisers:** red plate, white numbers.

National races have many more riders than Regionals do, and points are awarded accordingly:

Position	Moto	B Final	A Final
1	4	15	42
2	3.5	12	37
3	3	10	33
4	2	8	29
5	2	6	26
6	1	5	24
7	1	4	22
8	0.5	3	20

See the website of British Cycling (british-cycling.org.uk/bmx/article/bmxst_get_into) for more on points allocation.

With this points system, a rider is always awarded at least 1.5 points for competing in his or her three motos. This also helps riders who crash, as it ensures they receive at least some points.

National races receive a large amount of coverage from all aspects of the media. There are often many photographers and film cameramen in attendance, as well as the UK's premier BMX racing magazine *Twenty24 (2024)*, which has coverage of races all across the UK, Europe and the USA, as well as reviews and information on BMX racing. There is usually a report done by a British Cycling official that recounts the weekend's racing, and individual clubs may also do a report on how their own riders did.

A significant number of tracks in the UK are of National standard, but some still fall slightly short in terms of track upkeep,

COMPETITION STRUCTURE

facilities, parking or amenities. As a track will be used by such large numbers of riders, parents, teams and spectators over the course of an entire weekend, there needs to be a suitable amount of parking and space for tents and caravans.

Nationals are the races that attract the best riders in the country. As such, the competition level and fees are higher than almost any other type of race in the UK. Riders racing Nationals will usually be doing some sort of regular training off the bike (gym work, running, swimming, and so on) in order to raise all aspects of their fitness, resulting in much faster racing than at Regionals.

At the end of the season, official National titles are handed to those who have competed in at least eight of the rounds. The best eight results from the respective races (the rounds in which the rider scored the most points) are taken, added up, and then riders are placed according to who has the most points from their best eight rounds. This system of scoring emphasizes consistency, rather than luck.

It costs £15 for under-16s to race, £20 for over-17s and Junior Men, and £25 for Elite

Three riders during a race.

The crowd and food at a race meeting.

Men. This, coupled with the (variable) expense of travelling to and from the races, food and drink for the weekend and accommodation (among other things), makes Nationals very expensive, and not something to be taken lightly. While spectating can be great to get the motivation up, participation in National races should not be considered by anyone with less than a year's racing experience.

British Championships

The British Championships (or the Brits, as they are often referred to) are held across a single weekend (usually in September, once the National season has finished). Unlike National events, the titles are assigned after just one day of racing, so riders have to get everything right in all of their races if they want to reach the finals.

A normal sight during a race day.

COMPETITION STRUCTURE

The British Championships are run in order to crown a new British Champion across each of the categories, and proceed in a similar way to National events: there is a practice session followed by motos, quarter-finals, semi-finals, and a single A final to determine who takes home the title. This makes for very 'cut-throat' racing and, if you crash in the quarters, that is it for your event.

The Brits attract even larger numbers than Nationals, with the 2011 British Championships hosting a total 858 riders. There are very few tracks in the UK that can accommodate the number of people who take part in the Brits. Not only does the track have to be sufficiently well maintained to be able to withstand the sheer number of riders, races and practice sessions held over the course of the weekend, but it also has to have suitable areas for everyone to stay.

The Brits follow the same guidelines as the Nationals in terms of clothing: no excessively tight clothes and no helmets that do not cover the entire face and head.

Being the highest form of competition based solely in the UK (in other words, not Euro rounds, and so on), the Brits receive the most coverage. Every year photographers come from across the country, as well as videographers and British Cycling writers, and the Brits has even been broadcast on television.

To race at the Brits riders must have competed in a certain amount of Regional races. The requirement is usually just over half (five of eight, for example), but it can vary between regions. Riders who may have missed some races due to issues such as injury are able to apply for 'dispensation'.

The Brits are arguably the biggest event in the entire UK BMX calendar, and offer a chance for those who have perhaps under-performed at Nationals to prove their skills. They also provide the only opportunity for

Jumping is more dangerous but often faster than manualling or rolling.

The Manchester indoor track has wooden start hills.

regions and clubs to race against each other, and to find out which club has the best riders and which region has the fastest constituency. Riders race for their club and their region (usually wearing a race shirt handed to them for completing enough Regional races). After the races have finished, the points are added together to reveal which is the best.

It costs £20 to race in any category in the British Championships.

Euro Rounds

The UEC BMX European Series is run in the same way as the British National series, but across Europe instead of just Britain. There are around twelve rounds (two at each venue), held in countries throughout Europe, and entered by people of all nationalities, not just Europeans.

As with the Nationals, the categories are single age groups up to seventeen, then seventeen to twenty-four, twenty-five to twenty-nine, thirty plus, Junior Men and Elite Men. The women's is very similar, but with seventeen plus, Junior Women and Elite Women. The Euros also have Cruiser classes.

The rules for European standard tracks are much stricter than those relating to National level tracks, with each Euro track being restricted to between 300 and 400m long, with the start hill at least 1.5m high. The first straight has to be at least 40m long.

Euro rounds attract many more entrants than any race based solely in the UK. At one event in Kortrijk, Belgium in 2011, over 2110 registrations were made. This level of interest results in a massive amount of media coverage, not just from the UK scene, but also from BMXers overseas, as well as the presence of various vendors looking to expand their market. Since the UK has relatively few European-standard tracks, coverage of the Euro rounds in the UK tends to be restricted to magazines and word of mouth.

Due to the costs associated with racing a Euro round (travel to a different country for both rider and bike, food, drink, race fees, among other things), the vast majority of riders will be sponsored for at least part of their expenses.

Riders have to jump the pro section of a BMX track.

The World Championships

The first BMX World Championships took place in 1982. These Championships represent the highest level that any rider can reach without being professionally endorsed and trained. Held just once a year, they determine who is the best rider in the world across the different age categories.

Run in a similar way to the Brits, the World Championships take four days to complete. This includes practice, time trials, motos, quarter-finals, semi-finals, and the main final, as well as other events such as prize-givings,

WHO RUNS BMX INTERNATIONALLY?

The World Championships are run by UCI, which stands for Union Cycliste Internationale (International Cycling Union). Almost all international level races are run by UCI, with both the World Championships and the BMX Supercross being part of this. It also looks after other international-level cycling events such as 4X and downhill racing.

A Norwegian rider takes first place.

Girls as well as boys enjoy participating in BMX racing.

A sponsored rider will usually have their team's logo on their jersey and bike.

A rider covers his brake in the first corner.

warm-ups and registration. As with the one day of racing, there is no room for mistakes. Big favourites are not given any preferential treatment over other riders, so even if the 'guy to beat' is taken out in the first berm in the quarter-final, that is it for his title hopes. This makes the racing extremely exciting, as riders battle it out frantically to get up into the top four places in order to progress to the next tier of races.

The World Championships are a massive draw for BMX riders and fans alike. The 2011 World Championships held in Copenhagen drew 2200 riders and 18,000 spectators. The World Championships are also a major draw for the world's media. Almost every single BMX magazine, website, team and brand will be in attendance, along with some well-known news agencies and possibly even television crews, as well as websites to stream the action live online.

Supercross

Supercross BMX (also known as SX) is a far more extreme version of BMX racing. With 8m-high start hills, 40-foot jumps over berms and the occasional box jump, it is easy to imagine SX as BMX racing on steroids. Riders easily reach speeds of 40mph (65km/h) at the bottom of the wooden start hill, making it a version of the sport that is not for the faint-hearted.

The sprint to the first jump can be crucial for your race.

TAKE THIS FOR ME?

Because of the height of the start hills in Supercross and Olympic races, some riders have people to walk their bikes to the top for them. This saves their energy for the important part – the race itself.

Unlike the Worlds, SX is open only to Junior Men, Junior Women, Elite Men and Elite Women. This is because the standard (and complexity) of the tracks is simply too high for most riders, and sometimes not even the best riders in the world are able to tame the SX tracks.

Held in countries across the globe, the SX season has one race per track. Each event takes place over a weekend, with the practice sessions and time trials being held on the Friday and the races on the Saturday. Due to the number of riders who attend the SX races, time trials (each rider gets two attempts at riding the track by themselves to post the fastest time) are held to determine the fastest thirty-two (or sixty-four, depending on the organizers) riders. These riders then progress into the motos on the following day.

Tracks are designed by UCI track builder Tom Ritzenthaler, and are known for reflecting the extreme nature of BMX. Hip jumps (jumps where the landing is at a different angle to the take-off), box jumps (where the riders jump on to and off a metal box – imagine a

The winners of a Supercross race.

A rider holds his hand in the air after winning a race.

HOW LONG HAS BMX BEEN 'OFFICIAL'?

BMX racing has been a part of the UCI since 1993, and a part of the Olympics since 2008.

---

tabletop jump where there is a gap between the take-off and the table section), and even the famous berm jump.

SX races are some of the most widely covered in the entire calendar, and attract huge numbers of press, spectators and riders.

Only the best riders in the world can even think about riding these tracks, meaning that the vast majority (if not all) riders taking part will be completely sponsored. Race fees, bike parts, travel, food and any other costs associ-

---

THE FIRST OLYMPICS CHAMPION

The first-ever Elite Men's Olympic World Champion was Latvian Maris Strombergs. As well as taking the Olympic gold medal, he also won the World Championships several months earlier.

---

ated with taking part in the race will be paid for either by the sponsors or by the country for which they ride.

The Olympics

In August 2008 BMX finally got the respect it deserves, when the first-ever Olympic BMX race was held at the Beijing games in China. The day it became an officially recognized Olympic sport was a historic one for BMX. Twenty-one countries were represented in BMX in the 2008 Beijing Olympic Games, with eleven of them having riders in the finals. The first Olympic track was an SX-style track, with a berm jump and an 8m start hill.

The selection process for the Olympic Games is very complex, and not all riders are eligible. A country has to earn a spot in the Olympics, through points earned in UCI events. The countries with the most points are awarded a place, with a maximum of three spots being offered in the men's category and two spots in the women's. Countries then have their own selection process to determine which riders to put into those spots.

The Olympic tracks are the best-kept tracks in the world, and are completely purpose-built, being constructed a few months before the race, and then taken down afterwards. There is no public access to them because, while they may look fun, an under-skilled rider could seriously harm themselves if riding such a track without proper training and supervision.

Olympic BMX racing is watched by spectators throughout the world. The event at the 2008 Games was broadcast via eighteen cameras and covered by hundreds of reporters, photographers, magazines and other forms of media.

Sponsorship

As with any sport, there is sponsorship in BMX racing. A company/shop/individual will pay for a rider's parts, bike, and so on, as long as that rider carries their logo, and represents and spreads word of their organization. It is not on the same level as more mainstream sports, such as golf and Formula 1, where participants are sometimes paid million-dollar wages. BMX racers tend to be paid in parts and it is only the very top people in the sport (potential Olympic athletes) who receive financial recompense for their efforts.

Sponsorship is a goal of most riders as it not only gives financial help with racing, but also shows that companies have noticed a particular rider and become aware of his or her ability. This recognition is, to some riders, worth as much as the products they will be given. Inevitably, riders are more likely to be offered sponsorship the higher up the racing 'hierarchy' they go. Few companies will sponsor a rider who is not competing at least at

National level; these riders will, most likely, be racing at Regionals too.

Top athletes can expect multiple sponsors, with different companies providing different bike parts. For example, Maris Strombergs (who won the first Olympic gold for BMX racing) has received sponsorship from Freeagent, Rockstar, Kenda, Samox, Q2, ODI, Velo, UFO, THE, KMC and Sinz.

For someone just starting out in BMX racing, sponsorship will not be a concern. If and when you are good enough, sponsors will come. Some companies do advertise sponsorships through various channels (forums, websites, word of mouth, in BMX publications, and so on), so it can be worth keeping an eye out for any opportunities available once you have reached a certain level. Being a generally nice person is important for sponsors too – they do not want to sponsor someone who is not popular or respected, as this can help to influence what people buy.

Famous Riders

As with any sport, there are some competitors who are more famous than others. In BMX racing, some of the most high-level riders are;

Maris Strombergs
Also known as 'The Machine' (for his consistently fast riding and the number of wins he has), Strombergs has been at the very top of the sport since the 2008 World Championships. Having ridden for both One Bicycles and Freeagent, the Latvian rider moved out to California, USA, to train with Freeagent team manager (and BMX racing legend) Dale Holmes.

Kyle Bennett
American Kyle Bennett raced for over ten

Marcus Bloomfield.

years before his death in a motoring accident in 2012, and in this time earned the nickname 'Butter' for his smooth riding style. A multiple World Champion, he won championships in the USA, Canada and Australia.

Joris Daudet

2011 World and European Champion Joris Daudet is a French rider who has set the BMX world alight. Sponsored by GT and Oakley, among others, Daudet has taken wins all over the globe. He is one to watch out for.

Mike Day

Day is a (very tall) American rider, who turned pro at just seventeen years old. Sponsored by GT, he took the silver medal at the Beijing Olympics, and was the fastest person around the track in the time trials.

Donny Robinson

American Donny Robinson got the bronze medal at the 2008 Olympic games, then went on to win the 2009 Elite Men title at the World Championships. Standing at only 5ft 5in, Robinson has to work harder than the average rider, but what he lacks in height he makes up for in training.

Marc Willers

Marc Willers moved from his hometown in New Zealand to California in order to make a living in racing. With over twenty-two years in racing, and sponsors ranging from BOX Components to Burger King, Willers is always one to look out for at any SX race.

Shanaze Reade

British rider Shanaze Reade has been a World

Champion in both team sprint and BMX racing, and reached the final for BMX in the 2008 Olympic Games. Although recent years have seen old injuries flare up, she is always at the front of the pack when she races. Having been sponsored by such companies as Redline, GT and Oakley, Shanaze is currently one of the best female riders in the UK.

Marcus Bloomfield

British rider Marcus Bloomfield was the 2011 Elite Men's British Champion. He has raced in competitions all over the world, and is now involved in coaching, with British Cycling.

Sponsored by Fox and Shimano (among others), he is considered to be one of the nicest people in UK BMX.

Liam Phillips

Liam Phillips was the first-ever British rider to represent Britain at the Olympic Games in 2008. He even (by chance) had the honour to be the first BMX racer ever to compete in the Olympics – he was the first rider to post a time in the time trials. He races in almost all races, from the British National series upwards, and once took 2nd place in an SX race in Copenhagen.

The final of a Supercross race is always exciting.

CHAPTER 7

LEARNING TO RACE BMX AND TECHNIQUES

Coaching in BMX is as important to a competitor's improvement as it is in any other Olympic sport. While a natural progression can be seen from just riding the bike regularly, having a steady and well-structured coaching regime can help a rider to improve more quickly, seeing more noticeable results in a shorter time. This extends from club racing all the way up to the World Championships and Supercross races.

The information given here is intended to back up the advice given to you by a coach. Some coaches may give less information, while others will describe things very differently. There is no right or wrong in coaching, providing the pupil achieves the required

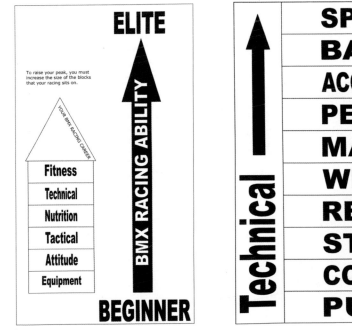

The BMX pyramid.

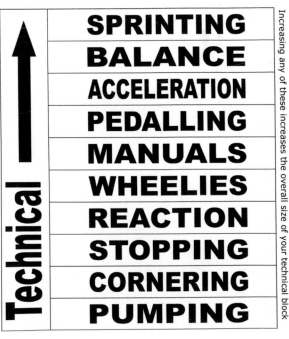

BMX skills.

result, safely and with the necessary under-standing.

The Purpose of Coaching and Training

Imagine your BMX career as pyramid – the tip of this pyramid is the best you can possibly be. The pyramid needs to be built on foundation blocks, which include such things as fitness, tactics, attitude and equipment. The most important block, however, is the one built on technique. BMX is possibly one of the most technically involved of all the main cycling disciplines, and mastering the core techniques is critical to success. The good news is that, while the other blocks require a certain level of maturity, techniques can be learned from a very early age. Many of them may be picked up even without access to a BMX track.

The diagrams show that an exceptional ability in one area can compensate for a lack in another. This is fairly realistic – if you cannot react when the gate drops but are a fantastic sprinter you will probably do all right. However, the very best riders will be good at both reacting and sprinting and anyone lacking in any area will be left behind. For this reason, it is important to practise your areas of weakness more than your strengths.

Club Coaching

While the advice here covers many of the core techniques, and aims to present them in a way that is helpful and will enable you to make progress, it cannot assess you as a rider, it cannot provide you with feedback while you practise, and it cannot deal with any accidents. Realistically, you will need to find yourself some sort of guide, too.

It is important to join a BMX racing club with a good coaching structure, with plenty of sessions available and a visible pathway for the progression of all its riders. At World Performance level riders have a team around them, who cover all the building blocks. A beginner will be concentrating on the tech-

A coach watches a rider through a berm.

Cones can be useful to plot the best lines.

niques, so will need a Level 2 BMX Coach. A coach of this level should be working with a club, providing coaching to groups of riders from beginner to intermediate level. Depending on the type of club or team, some more advanced aspects of racing should be covered. As riders progress and the coaching sessions become more advanced, the groups generally need to be smaller. Riders will need to

earn their place in these smaller groups by demonstrating competence in the core techniques. The coach should make an assessment of every rider, by observing them on the track and when racing, so that he or she can teach at a level that those riders are able to handle.

Every coach will be slightly different, but there are a few key points that determine whether coaching is any good:

- Are you enjoying the sessions?
- Do you understand why your coach is asking you to do the activities?
- Do you think your riding is improving?
- Is your coach giving personal and specific feedback that you understand? (This may be provided as a general observation to the group, but given in such a way that you know you are one of the riders who needs the information.)
- Do you feel you can ask questions?

KNOW YOUR TERMINOLOGY

The terms 'skill' and 'technique' will be used here, with the following definitions: a technique is mastered when the rider has learned to ride a particular way; the skill lies in knowing when to ride that way and in being able to do so when necessary.

A coach addresses riders.

- Is the coach willing to provide information on his or her qualifications and CPD? Is it being updated regularly?

Coaching methods and delivery are continually changing, and a good coach will be keeping up with the latest information. This means gradual changes should be evident, such as new ideas being tried out. New activities may not work as intended, but if this happens the coach should be able to explain this to the group so the riders at least understand the intention of the session even if it failed.

Once you join the club and start to attend the coached sessions, your coach will probably tell you to go away and practise. While this may seem contradictory to the advice that you must find a club and coach, the key point here is to 'practise', not to 'go away'. Many of the core techniques for BMX are very similar to those for any cycling discipline and should ideally be practised away from the track in a safe (or at least safer) environment. Clearly, this is the only possible way to learn. A BMX track is made up of obstacles for the rider to overcome, but he or she first needs to acquire the technique and skills to deal with those obstacles.

Riders who learn only on the track learn to ride their bike on that track, instead of learning to ride a BMX bike on any BMX track. They may well win on the track they know, but may suddenly find themselves simply making up the numbers when taken to a different track or faced with a rider who can ride the track differently.

There are a few simple and easy steps to take on the route to becoming the best BMX racer you can possibly be:

1. Joining the club.
2. Attending plenty of the available sessions.
3. Learning from the coach.
4. Learning from other riders.
5. Ensuring you spend as much of the rest of your time as you can riding and practising.

It is very important to do more than simply learn the core techniques and then move on. For their whole career, all riders must keep returning to these techniques and practising them. At the higher levels of cycling, or indeed any sport, the difference between winning and losing becomes smaller and smaller, even down to a thousandth of a second. Being slightly better at one of the core techniques

A Talent-Team rider jumping.

could give you the thousandth of a second that you need to win. If you become a thousandth of a second faster in five techniques, you are winning by five thousandths of a second. This concept is known as 'marginal gains', a term that is used by Olympic and World Class coaches in many sports. This is extremely advanced and a long way from the point at which a novice enters the sport, but future gains to the highest level may only be achieved if the basics are learned, practised and continually improved. The younger the rider, the easier it is for them to learn.

Any description of the theory behind a particular technique has been kept short and simple and is included only where it might be helpful to your understanding and learning. Do not worry if you struggle with the theory on its own; just concentrate on the description of the techniques themselves.

You and Your Bike

In BMX racing the extent to which you can interact with and control your bike is absolutely critical. You can simply ride the track over and over again, but this will only make you very good at riding that particular track. There is a much better way, and that is to learn the core techniques away from the track. Not only does this let you practise them in isolation, it will also allow you to practise them much more often.

Isolation means practising a single technique by itself, eliminating other techniques that usually have to be carried out at the same time or closely together. It does not really mean practising alone. For your safety, you should always ensure as much as possible that you are riding in groups.

In order to take full control of your bike,

Checking your bike before riding is essential.

Riders balancing on the gate.

you must understand how it moves, and how you can interact with it. For BMX racing, there are a finite number of actions that the bike will need to be able to accomplish:

- Remaining stationary when you are balanced on the gate.
- Moving forwards, when pedalling or just rolling.
- Leaning left or right to turn.
- Steering, at slower speeds, by turning the bars.
- Rising, any time the bike is moving upwards.

- Dropping, any time the bike is moving downwards.

It is not just the bike that can move; the rider can too. Assuming that at all times his or her feet stay on the pedals, the rider's actions can be summarized as follows:

- stationary (the neutral position);
- moving forwards, leaning over the front of the bike;
- moving backwards, over the back of the bike;

A rider leaning and turning their bike.

ABOVE: A rider pushing their weight forwards.

RIGHT: A rider pushing their weight backwards.

- moving to the side, either with the bike, or against it to maintain control;
- folding; allowing the bike to move up without you moving up;
- extending, the bike being allowed or made to drop without you also dropping.

By combining one or more bike actions with one or more rider actions, all the required techniques for BMX racing can be accomplished. It is important to remember this explanation when working through all the techniques that need to be learned.

A rider's actions can be passive (where they are letting the bike move them), active (where they are making the bike do something), and neutral (where they are moving without considering the bike). For example, when a bike rolls over an obstacle, a rider will passively fold, allowing the bike to rise. Then, at the top, they can either actively

extend by pushing the bike down the other side (see 'Pumping') or they can neutrally extend by 'popping' off the bike, causing the bike to follow them into the air (see 'Jumping'). However, trying to put all of a rider's actions into these exact slots does not quite work.

For shorter definitions for the terms that are used in coaching, see page 131, but do remember that different coaches describe methods and techniques in different ways. What one coach may refer to as 'folding' may be described by another as 'compressing', or 'sucking it up'.

Learning the techniques will take practice. Everyone will be different, with some riders becoming very good at some techniques more quickly than others. It is vital to dedicate more practice to your weaker areas, but you must still practise those that you are good at – even Olympic athletes regularly practise the core techniques. Elite-level competitions are won by a fraction of a second, so the slightest gain made by being fractionally better at one of the core techniques can be the difference between winning and losing.

The Techniques

When working with a group of eight riders, it is very easy for a coach to identify weaknesses when those riders attempt a new technique. From the pages of a book this sort of assessment is impossible, so anyone trying to learn in this way will have to be very honest with themselves.

The descriptions of BMX-specific skills given here will be about the perfect model, along with steps to take to achieve that model, as well as an indication of common mistakes made when learning.

The Saddle Push

Although not exactly related to BMX (other than perhaps looking cool when walking with your bike), this first simple technique is intended to demonstrate the learning process, to help you to understand this process and how to use it for the rest of the techniques.

Stand on the left of the bike. Hold the saddle in your left hand and put your right hand by your side. The challenge is to push the bike forwards, maintaining as straight a line as you can. Try it a few times and you will quickly improve. But how has this happened?

On your first attempt the bike was all over the place. On the second attempt you slowed it down to see what was going on. On the third attempt you start leaning the bike to compensate for the wild steering; by the fourth, fifth, sixth (and more) attempts, you were learning to compensate more quickly, and speeding up. If you continue to practise, your reactions will improve; there will be less conscious thought about your actions. Eventually it will appear to everyone else that you can miraculously push your bike in a perfectly straight line using just the saddle.

This is the process for learning all the techniques:

- **Unconsciously incompetent** – you had no idea that a bike can even be pushed by the saddle.
- **Consciously incompetent** – you know that a bike can be pushed by the saddle, but you are not very good at doing it.
- **Consciously competent** – with care and at slow speeds you can succeed with the technique.
- **Unconsciously competent** – you can succeed with the technique without having to consciously think about it.

With a technique as seemingly simple as the saddle push (but is it that simple?), within a very short time you will reach the consciously

DON'T FORGET

Even when you are unconsciously competent at a technique, continual practice is still required, though perhaps a bit less than for those techniques that you are not as good at.

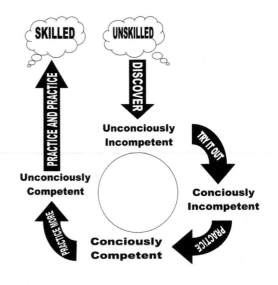

The learning cycle.

competent or even unconsciously competent state. There are no shortcuts to this learning cycle, and the length of time it will take to complete the cycle for each technique will vary depending on complexity, how well you can master the techniques on which it is built, and of course your natural ability on the bike. Everything can be learned, but with some techniques some riders will simply be better than others.

Riders on the gate.

From the top view of rider balanced against a wall

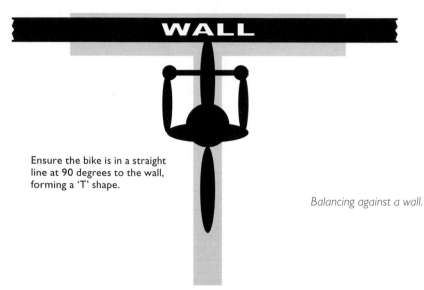

Ensure the bike is in a straight line at 90 degrees to the wall, forming a 'T' shape.

Balancing against a wall.

Balancing

At the start of a BMX race, the riders line up behind the gate. After the 'voice start sequence' the gate will drop and the race begins. To ensure the fastest start, a rider needs to be able to balance his or her bike with the front wheel against the gate while standing on both pedals. Stability is important here. If the gate drops and you are leaning left, you will exit the gate moving left. (Your experiment with the saddle push will have told you that, when your bike leans left, it turns left.)

The startpad – the area behind the gate on which your bike sits – will be on an angle sloping down to the gate. To practise your balancing you need to find a wall, fence or kerb that is on a similar slope, against which you can place your wheel. Ensure the bike is in a straight line at 90 degrees to the wall, forming a 'T' shape.

Level your pedals, so that the trailing pedal (the one towards the back of the bike) is in

line with the chainstay (the bar running from the middle of the pedals to the middle of the back wheel). Stand over the bike holding the bars, place your foot on the leading pedal (the one towards the front), stand on this and bring your other foot to the trailing pedal. Keep practising this until the bike no longer immediately falls to the side; or at least you are able to remain on the bike, even if you are wobbling.

There is no such thing as a perfectly balanced bike. It is all about continual adjustment and correction. If the bike falls left, lean slightly right and pull up with your left arm. As you get better, you should be able to react more quickly to smaller movements. Start using just your shoulders to correct the bike. Instead of pulling on the left you can push on the right. Eventually, at least to the onlooker, you will appear to be perfectly balanced.

Once you have a bit of balance, you need to be able to change position easily. Many clubs will run on-gate exercises to help you to practise this. You will probably be asked to do such actions as sitting down, standing up, leaning back, leaning forwards, one-handed, one-footed, nudging the rear wheel left and right, and spinning the pedals. Older and more experienced riders using clipless pedals will be asked to clip and unclip from the pedals.

For the correct body position for a BMX start, the arms should be slightly bent and held strong, with wrists straight or ever so slightly rolled over. Both legs will be slightly bent, and you should be slightly further back than your saddle – but not too far. If your back is nice and straight you are in the correct position. As it is impossible to see your own back, a friend is useful here.

If your coach is present they will be continually correcting your position, but will only consider one little bit at a time and wait for you to get used to that before moving on to the next area.

Keep your head up and looking forwards – remember you will ride towards what you are looking at. Contrary to the instruction given by the voice start, do not watch the gate. If you are using the lights you need to watch them using your peripheral vision and not looking directly at them.

The most common mistakes seen on the start gate are:

- touching the saddle;
- being too far back;
- having your wrists rolled under, or too far over;
- looking down at the gate, or looking at the lights.

The perfect gate stance.

Starting (Key Technique)

Within BMX, riders and coaches always talk about practising starts. A gate start involves the following:

- Balancing on the gate.
- Reacting to the gate dropping.
- Accelerating.

There really is nothing more to it than that.

Acceleration

Acceleration means increasing the speed of your bike, and in BMX this is almost always sudden and 'explosive'. Not only do you want to be going faster, but you also need to be going faster immediately.

Acceleration is based on an awful lot of physics. At this level, though, the theory may be simplified to a few easy statements (with some terms not being used in a strictly scientific sense):

TRAIN SMART

This is an 'either/and' situation, so you can apply one of the beneficial changes, or many of them. The one caveat to this is that care must be taken if you are training for strength (which should only be done by adult riders anyway). If it is done wrong, the gain in strength will be negated by a decrease in speed and an increase in weight. If you decide that you need to gain strength, get expert advice. A Level 2 BMX coach cannot provide this help unless they also hold further suitable qualifications outside of cycling.

Riders on the ODP (Olympic Development Programme) are the best in the country.

A rider in the neutral position.

1. A given amount of power applied to an object makes it move at a given speed, and the greater the power is over the weight the faster the speed.
2. Power is comprised of strength and speed.
3. A moving object continues moving until stopped by resistance.

This means that, for each turn of your pedal (the application of power), you will move the combined weight of yourself and your bike (the object) up to a certain speed, and that, once it is moving, it will keep moving until slowed back down.

As a result of this, in order to accelerate at a faster rate you need to increase your strength or speed, or decrease your weight or resistance.

Accelerating technique can be practised on any flattish ground. Pedal up to a speed around jogging pace, then get in the neutral position – pedals horizontal, standing over the saddle, tall on the bike – and let the bike roll.

Begin pedalling as hard and as fast as you can, and keep going for 10 seconds. Here you have applied power to the bike. Return to the neutral position; allow the bike to slow back down until you are rolling at jogging pace again. This time, as you begin pedalling also move your body forwards on the bike. This forward position should only last for one pedal revolution, after which you should have naturally returned to the centre of the bike. By moving your body forwards you have done two key things:

1. As your body is already moving, your pedal stroke needs to accelerate only the bike, effectively making you lighter.
2. As your weight is over the front, resistance on the back tyre is reduced, allowing it to accelerate more easily. You can only

go so far with this, as you need a certain amount of resistance for your tyre to grip. 'Wheel spin' will not get you moving. Wet or loose ground, or worn tyres, will affect how likely you are to suffer wheel spin.

To get the best effect of using your body weight to lighten the bike, it has to be a quick, sudden movement. Imagine you are trying to surprise your bike. You should learn it slowly, but you will not notice the effect until you are confident enough to throw your weight forwards quite aggressively.

As your body naturally returns to neutral, you can repeat the forward surge for the second pedal. Timing is critical to get the best effect for this, so it must be practised regularly.

There are many issues that can have a negative effect on acceleration, some of which are easier to resolve than others:

- Poorly maintained bike – stiff bearings or rubbing brakes increase the resistance.
- Poor pedal technique decreases the amount of power that can be applied.
- An unsuitably sized bike or components decreases the amount of power that can be applied.
- Tyre size and type can increase or decrease resistance, so these must be chosen to

---

INVESTING IN YOUR HEALTH

Until maturity children are unable significantly to increase their strength, and any attempts to do this may be damaging. However, there is research that has shown that children who regularly compete in sports that require fast muscle work will develop a higher proportion of 'fast-twitch' fibres within the muscles used.

---

match the requirements. Thankfully most tyres are now general purpose so the days of swapping tyres have mostly gone.

A productive and beneficial training session suitable for all ages might involve accelerating repeatedly over a short distance, or accelerating then sprinting for distances of about 80m. This sort of practice will condition the body to ride using sudden 'explosive' power, as well as improving aerobic recovery (the ability to recover more quickly after a sustained effort). For older, mature riders it will also increase strength and speed and, therefore, power.

Starting Out of the Gate

Starting out of the BMX gate involves adding a few techniques together: balancing in the start position, then, when the gate drops, accelerating out. The exact point at which you need to begin accelerating is dependent on the gate itself, and is something you will have to learn at each track. As you become more experienced it will become easier to adapt to different gates. Another thing to remember is that a change of bike or equipment will also affect your start point, as will your development, as you get stronger.

The starting procedure (group of techniques) is as follows:

- Balance on the gate, in the start position.

TYRE TYPES

A few years ago the pros would be seen slicing the knobs off knobbly tyres in an attempt to match the amount of grip they wanted to the track surface and conditions. Improvements in tyre design, materials and cost now mean the right tyre is usually available off the shelf, and for most riders the single tyre type is fine.

- Make sure you are looking where you want to be riding.
- As you start, move your body forwards and begin to pedal.
- Keep your arms strong and the bike straight.
- If you are strong enough, the front of the bike will slightly lift. You can use this to your advantage to start slightly earlier and allow the front wheel to float over the falling gate.
- As your second pedal comes round, your body should have returned to neutral - repeat the body forward action for the second pedal. Do this smoothly, to avoid any jerkiness.

There are a few common mistakes made by riders at the start:

- Starting too far back on the bike.
- 'Ducking' instead of moving the whole body forwards.
- Pulling the bike upwards.
- Forcing the bike to roll backwards.
- Looking at the lights, or at other riders.

Your start is one of the most important parts of the race. The faster you can start the better your position will be on the track. Remember that the winner of a BMX race is not the fastest rider but the first over the line. A good start can put you at the front and lets you pick your favourite line – preferably the fastest. You will be able to protect your inside on the corners, and all the riders behind you will have to either stay behind you or take wider, riskier lines. Being in control of the race in this way is crucial and means that even riders who are technically faster than you will be unable to overtake.

Unfortunately, this crucial part of racing can only be practised at the BMX track, so it is important to use the time at weekly gate practice sessions wisely. The rest of the time can be used to practise acceleration using the roll in and sprint method.

Advanced Off-Track Gate Practice
There are two further methods to practise start technique. The first is to purchase a single-man training gate. These range from a simple wooden 'roll back to drop' version to

A magnetic practice gate.

*A rider balancing
on the block.*

a complete pneumatic version with voice box and timing system. Although it is of course the ideal way to practise gates away from the track, this sort of equipment represents a significant investment and requires a lot of space.

The second method is slightly more accessible. While not covering all the aspects of a gate start, it does allow you to practise accelerating from stationary. It involves using a block to rest your rear pedal on, and 'balancing' the bike by just slightly keeping your weight on the rear pedal. The block must be at the correct height, and the pedal must be positioned so that as you ride away your foot

*A rider setting off from
the block.*

A block can be a useful way to practise gate starts away from the track.

will not hit the block. This balance position is slightly different from that used on the gate, so it is important only to transfer just enough weight to the rear pedal to maintain stability.

Having established your position, you can now accelerate away from the block. To work on your reactions have a helper provide start triggers (such as a whistle) or prepare some recordings of the voice start on an MP3 player. This is an ideal way to practise acceleration from stationary because you have removed the balancing aspect and so you are practising accelerating in 'isolation'. Finding ways to practise techniques on their own like this will allow you many more opportunities to train and develop.

A block can be made of any material, as long as it is the correct height.

Sprinting (Key Technique)

In terms of sprinting and pedal technique, there are three common mistakes made by most riders:

- Having the wrong part of the foot in contact with the pedal.
- Pedalling by pushing downwards on the pedals. This is known as 'chopping' and causes slight pauses while the cranks are vertical. It is not efficient.
- Swinging the bike from side to side while sprinting. The bike should go forwards only.

If the point of sprinting is to travel as fast as you can (and it really is), then you have to make sure as much of the power you can provide is transferred to the rear wheel. This must also be done as efficiently as possible, to produce maximum power and reduce fatigue. There is no point having great amounts of power if it is all wasted and you get too tired to complete the race.

Foot Position and Movement

For most people, when walking, the foot is arched and contact is made with the ground with only the heel and the ball. As a result, these are the toughest parts of the foot, with the least soft flesh to absorb some of the power created, but enough to absorb most of the shocks. As balance is also an important part of BMX and the rider needs to be able to pivot the feet, the ball of the foot should be used for pedalling. The foot should be positioned so that the pedal axle (the centre part on which the pedal spins) is directly under the ball of the foot.

Many youngsters seem to prefer using the bridge of the foot, usually because it feels more stable when they first learn to ride. This position dramatically reduces the movement available to the foot and ankle, and in most shoes there will be a gap or a layer of soft comfy foam between sole and foot at this point that has to be compensated for – meaning wasted power.

The pedals do not work up and down but rather in a circle. When pedalling you need to think of these circles. When practising pedal technique, always start slowly and build up speed during the training session. The art of pedalling relies on the flexibility of the foot and ankle and the quality of grip between pedal and shoe. The actual pedalling action can be defined, but only a slow-motion video will verify that it is happening:

1. Pedal at 12 o'clock, foot level, pushing forwards.
2. Pedal at 2 o'clock, heel dropping, pushing down.
3. Pedal at 4 o'clock, heel rising, pushing down.
4. Pedal at 6 o'clock, foot level, scraping back.
5. Pedal at 8 o'clock, heel rising, scraping up.
6. Pedal at 10 o'clock, heel dropping, passive.

The 'scraping' action is similar to the way in which you might clean up your shoe on grass after treading in something unpleasant. With cheaper pedals with cast pins, or shoes without suitably soft soles for the pins to grip, the scraping action needs to be relaxed, as this is the point at which the foot is more likely to slip off the pedal. If you do have good grippy pedals then you should find your heel rising on the upstroke significantly more than it drops for the downstroke.

PEDALLING PROBLEMS

If the bike is swinging side to side or the rider is having to lean side to side even at slower speeds, this is probably a sign that the crank is too long.

PEDAL POWER

Your pedal is the main point of power transfer between you and the bike. Investing in a decent set of pedals and using them correctly will improve your bike riding way more than any other upgrade. Expect to pay 10–20 per cent of the value of the bike for good pedals.

The good news is that if you have your feet positioned on the pedal correctly, and you pedal using circles instead of chopping, any side-to-side movement of the bike should be almost eliminated. All that is needed now to keep yourself nice and straight and travelling in the direction you want to be are some very slight corrections – as the right pedal moves between top and bottom, just pull up slightly on the right side of the handlebars. As when you are balancing on the gate, this should be done using your shoulders and not your arms. If pulling on the right is not enough, then push with the left at the same time. When viewed from the front your shoulders should be seen rolling in time as your legs pedal the bike.

Sprinting should be practised away from the track in sprint training sessions. You do not need to try to do everything all at once. Practise a single thing, slowly at first then speed it up. Then practise something else. Then try combining a couple together.

Of course, it is impossible to see yourself while doing this. If you are working on getting some or all of these techniques correct you will need somebody to watch you and provide you with feedback.

Stopping

The BMX bike has evolved to be perfect for handling many of the technical challenges imposed on it, but still it is not very good at stopping. Many BMX street and dirt riders do not have a brake at all, and neither is a brake used in most cycling sprint disciplines. However, a BMX race bike must have at least a single rear brake fitted. A rear brake is useless for stopping quickly, and is mostly there simply to slow the bike down if necessary. Again this is all down to bike control and must be mastered by the rider.

There is no front brake on a BMX bike because if it were to be pulled hard during a race, it would stop only the front wheel, thereby stopping the front of the bike but not the back. This would result in the rider going over the handlebars, which is not something that should be happening.

CORNERING TECHNIQUE

Sometimes, sliding while cornering can be kept under control, and in the early BMX days of flat, loose corners this was sometimes a useful tactic. However, modern tracks have bowled berms for corners, often made from tarmac. Sliding on these will not do the tyres any good, or provide any real advantage. Most clubs will frown upon riders skidding around their tracks.

The brake itself acts only on the wheel, attempting to bring it to a stop. If you do this suddenly, and the tyre does not have enough grip on the ground, then traction will be lost and you will slide. If your bike is sliding you are not in control.

To gain the most stopping power from the brake, you must apply it with just enough force not to lock the back wheel. Unfortunately, the level of force will vary depending on surface, conditions and brake wear. Feathering the brake – increasing your braking to

Jumping over a bar can tell you how high you can jump.

maximize the stopping force, then releasing before the wheel locks up – can be extremely effective if you remember. If you do forget and the wheel locks up, simply release the brake to regain grip and maintain control, then reapply, just like feathering.

One other action that will assist in slowing the bike is moving your weight backwards over the rear wheel. This increases the force keeping the wheel in contact with the ground, increasing the resistance between the two surfaces. This will allow you to brake harder before the wheel begins to lock up.

Finally, always brake in a straight line. A turning bike has a myriad of forces acting on it already and is only just maintaining contact with the ground. If you lock your rear wheel as well during such a manoeuvre the bike will simply slide out from under you.

Practising this is simple. Start riding slowly and brake. See how long it takes you to stop. Repeat from about the same speed but moving your weight over the back wheel – you should stop more quickly. Keep repeating this from faster speeds and get used to it.

You really want stopping to become a habit – you need to be unconsciously competent in the technique. If you ever have to use it on a BMX track it will be in an emergency and probably while you are thinking about a different technique. You do not want to be having to think in detail about stopping or slowing down when it is urgent that you do so.

Coaches will generally tell you to stay off the brake. Their job is to improve your competence and ability on the track, but a good coach should explain and run the odd session covering braking. It is generally better to stop safely if you have to and still have a chance to race again, rather than crashing and getting injured.

While you should not need to use the brake until the end of the race, you should get used to riding while 'covering' the brake. The brake on your BMX should be set up so that you can apply it with a single finger, while also being able to transfer more fingers quickly. Practise moving your index finger over the brake lever and back, moving your other fingers on and off the lever. This is fairly natural if you have been riding a bike for a while. As a BMX bike only has one brake, you need to decide which side you would prefer to have the lever. In the UK the rear brake is usually on the left, but if you regularly ride other bikes you will probably find you do a lot of your major braking with your right hand. There is no reason why you cannot have your BMX brake on the right.

Maintaining Speed

Once you can start and stop, and are producing as much speed as you can when pedalling, you need to look at maintaining that speed around a BMX track. A BMX track is generally not suitable for pedalling all the way around.

The main method of maintaining speed is still pedalling. A successful BMX racer will be able to switch between not pedalling and pedalling as hard and fast as they can almost instantly, and keep increasing the speed until they are 'spinning' the pedals. Once again this is something that just has to be practised, but it fits nicely into the sprint training session.

The speed at which a rider can pedal is affected by a number of factors. Some of these are physiological – such as strength or build – and some are equipment-related, such as bike size, crank length and gearing. Gearing on a BMX is the ratio between the chainring and the freewheel, and is the subject of much debate in the BMX community. The longer the gear (bigger front/smaller rear), the further the bike travels for each turn of the pedals, but the harder it is to make the turn. Increasing the crank-arm length may make it feel easier, but then the legs are moving further so it may be less comfortable.

BMX BY NUMBERS

Say one power can make one weight move one distance and the gearing means this is done in one turn, changing the gearing may mean that it still takes one power to make one weight move one distance, but now it may only take half a turn.

At this level, it is not necessary to consider the gearing in too much detail. Unless you find it extremely hard to pedal, or you are regularly unable to pedal effectively because the bike is going too fast ('spinning out'), it can be left alone. If you do make changes, make them slowly, changing the front chainring one tooth at a time. If it is too hard to pedal, decrease the front chainring. If you regularly 'spin out', then increase the front chainring.

Pumping (Key Technique)

Pumping is a key technique, which allows the rider to maintain and even increase speed when the frequency of the obstacles means that pedalling is not possible. It is learned initially on the rhythm section of the track, which should have been designed and built to maximize the technique.

The simplest way to describe pumping is to say that it is the act of pushing the bike forwards using your arms and legs. To do this you need to be crouched on the bike with bent arms and legs. The position is referred to here as 'folded', but other coaches may refer to it as 'compressed' or 'crouched' or 'sucked up'. Then you extend by pushing the bike away from you in a forward direction. You can practise this to a certain extent on a slight downhill slope, or on the flat by trying to do it around a slalom course.

When practising in this way it is mostly the arms that are being used. However, because of the small frame and low saddle on a BMX bike, the legs can play a much bigger role, especially on the track. It is not so easy to push your bike forwards using your legs but you can certainly push it downwards, and if this is done on the back of a jump it will also move it forwards. If timed correctly over a rhythm section, the combination of forwards with your arms and downwards with your legs can generate exceptional speed.

Pumping Exercise – Forwards on the Flat

On a slight downhill slope with the bike just rolling, lean forwards and bend your arms so that your chest is close to the handlebars. Then push the bike forwards and away from you, as soon as your arms are fully extended. Repeat. You should notice a small momentum gain, but nothing too huge.

Pumping Exercise – The Slalom

In a slalom, the riders weave around a series of low objects, such as sports markers, using

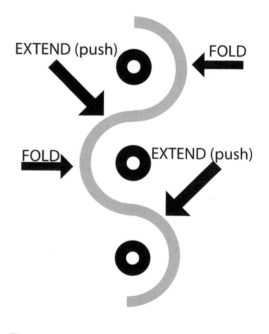

The pumping slalom course.

A rider pumping.

the pumping technique. The bike will be leaning as you turn, and you have to time the pump action to correspond with the exit of each turn. Because of the forces involved in turning, this gives you slightly more to pump against, and can generate high speeds. This is because, rather than just pushing forwards, you will be pushing round.

It is difficult to explain, but once you have a go you should get the feel for it. This exercise also has a secondary purpose, for cornering.

Pumping on the Track

It is difficult to give a detailed explanation of pumping exercises because pumping is very much about feel, and the specific timings for the combination of you and your bike have to be learned by trial and error. Keep practising it whenever you can. After just a few goes you will realize that the timing is critical. If you pump too early or too late, you will lose momentum instead of maintaining or gaining it. Once you move on to the rhythm section of the track, you will want to start using your legs much more, which will provide much more energy into the pump. On top of that, you can use the energy in the momentum of

the bike to bend your arms and legs instead of wasting your own.

As the bike rises over the jump, you relax and fold your arms and legs so the bike rises into you. Your pedals will need to be horizontal. As the bike passes the top of the jump, you are ideally positioned to push the bike out and get that desired pump. Try to imagine watching yourself from the side – while the bike moves up and down over the jump, your head stays in the same line.

You will find that your arms will push out naturally when they need to. The aim is to keep the front wheel on the ground, so you will push slightly more down than forwards. However, on the back of a jump the shape of the track will transfer this downward force into forward momentum. A fraction of a second later, it will be time to push with the legs. You need to practise the timing to determine when to push with your legs. If you get the timing right you will build up significant speed; it can be quite surprising the first time you achieve it!

There is a lot to think about with pumping, but this is a massive part of racing and well worth the time spent practising. Every track will have at least one section where the optimum race tactic is to pump, yet every track will be slightly different. Club coaches often use pump races to enforce this learning, expecting their students to negotiate all or part of the track without pedalling.

Cornering

Cornering in BMX is very different from cornering in most other forms of cycling.

Berms are good for overtaking.

Much of it relates to tactics and is something to consider only as your career progresses. However, there are some basics that must be covered.

The corner of a BMX track will usually be 180 degrees, banked and bowled. Its job is to keep the riders on the track and almost to 'slingshot' them around to where they want to be. The shape is very specific – the faster you go, the more you need to lean and the higher up the 'bowl' you go. This keeps your bike at about 90 degrees to the track with as much traction as possible. If you go too high too slowly, you will slide out. If you go too low too fast, you will slide out. The challenge is to be as low as possible as fast as possible.

One of the other key factors to note is the size of these turns. The very outside of the turn can be three times longer than the inside. For three turns of a 12m radius, if you take the very outside of each turn, you will ride almost 50m extra in the race compared with a rider who takes the inside of each turn.

If you are cornering at speed at the correct height and lean for that speed, you can continue pedalling around the turn. However, it is unwise to get into this habit. It is better to keep your pedals in the neutral position, to avoid the chance of them catching the ground and to ensure that you are ready to pedal out of the turn.

PRACTICE AND PREPARATION

Just as you become a better rider by riding more, you become a better racer by racing more. However you must decide which races are about practice and training, and which are about winning. Smaller club races, especially those that try to match on ability rather than age, are ideal for this. You must challenge yourself though – an easy win is of no benefit to your training.

The race line around a turn is rarely the fastest, but it is the one that protects you from being overtaken on the inside. This re-emphasizes the importance of being the first out of the gate and taking control of the race. You must enter the turn as quickly as you can, as close to the inside as you can. Once in the turn, allow the bike to turn as it needs to. If you are going at the correct speed, this should take you across the berm to exit on the far side.

The rider behind you now has two choices. They can follow you around, or they can enter the berm a little wider, go a little higher and try to overtake you on your inside. This is known as the high-low line. If you enter the berm side by side at the same speed you will exit side by side at the same speed.

Corners are the place where most over-taking takes place in BMX races. Cornering can be practised only on a BMX track, so this is another important area on which to spend your precious track time. Practise both the main lines on the different corners at various speeds. You also need to practise them

in groups, especially in the first turn, where there could be eight riders entering at the same time. Unfortunately, it is difficult to replicate this situation in anything other than a formal race environment. Enter as many races as possible, and accept that some races are more about practice than about competition.

Leaving the Ground – One Wheel at a Time

One of the things you will need to do in BMX is leave the ground. You will probably do this accidentally at first, before learning to manual over some of the doubles on the track. However, being able to manual a double on a track does not mean you can manual. As with

Manualling can be quicker than pumping.

all the techniques, it is important to learn how to do it properly, and to practise it until you have full control over your balance, speed and distance. Once you can do this, you should be able to manual any section of any track.

The wheelie – when you lift the front wheel and pedal for a distance – is the easiest of the two methods of lifting the front wheel. The technique involves suddenly starting a strong pedal action while moving your body over the back of the bike. As the front of the bike lifts you reach the balance point and continue pedalling.

The manual is a little more difficult. You are lifting the bike without the help of the pedal, so you will need to move further back – closer to the point of no return. One of the reasons it is easier to manual on the track is because the track itself has a 'lip' on the jumps that kicks your front wheel up, giving you extra assistance.

Avoiding Accidents

Raising your front wheel requires a certain amount of confidence, and perhaps a little bit of faith in your own ability. It is natural to be worried about going too far and landing on your back. Quite right too – if it happens it will hurt for a while. There are two ways to avoid this sort of accident. First, cover the brake and, if the bike is moving forwards and you feel you are going too far back, give it a quick dab. This will instantly return the bike to two wheels. You must avoid applying the brake while trying to lift the front wheel though. This should not be a problem as there should be no real force applied to the bars.

The second way to avoid an accident is simply to jump off the back of the bike. Actually jumping off a moving bike on to the stationary ground, both feet at once, takes a bit of practice. Stepping off – one foot at a time – is a little easier and provides more control for the landing.

TIPS FOR GETTING THE FRONT WHEEL UP

When first learning to lift the bike using the pedal to assist, bringing the bike almost to a standstill before the 'rocking action' can help.

You can practise both these methods. First, to familiarize yourself with stepping off the back of your bike, find a slightly uphill area (on grass just in case it goes wrong). You need to be rolling up the hill at about walking pace with your lead pedal at about 2 o'clock. Then, in a quick movement, slightly compress your arms, so your body moves slightly forwards, then move back quickly and at the same time start pedalling. Think of it as trying to 'surprise' your bike. It thinks all your weight is going to the front, then suddenly it is all at the back and the front is light enough to lift.

When the front wheel lifts, it may not be very far at first, so you either need to move further back or move more quickly. Do not try to pull up on the bars, as this is unnecessary and in reality is impossible. However, as your arms straighten and you lock them up at near straight this will have a slight pull effect.

Once the bike is lifting high enough and feels like it is going all the way, take the foot that was on the trailing pedal off the bike and on to the floor. This moves your weight even further back and the bike will continue rising. Once your foot is on the floor remove the other and come to a stop. You should now be standing on the ground, holding your handlebars with the bike upright.

Keep practising this until you can do it each time you try, at various speeds (not too fast), and on the flat and downhill. Do not remove your foot from the pedal until you have to. If you take it off too early you will upset your left to right balance. Remember this is supposed

Jumping backwards off a bike.

to be an emergency recovery when it all goes wrong.

Once you are happy that you can step off the back, practise the brake method. Use exactly the same method of lifting the bike, but then, instead of taking your foot off the pedal, a quick pull of the brake will return your bike to the ground. Do not keep the brake on too long or you will land very hard. Remember to move your body forwards as well, so you land in the neutral position.

Finally, try to return the bike to the ground simply by moving your weight forwards again. Depending how far back you are, this may not be easy.

Wheelies

Using exactly the same method to lift the bike (see above), try to continue pedalling. You need to be ready to step off the back

or dab your brake, but continuing to pedal should mean that you naturally remain slightly further forwards in a more balanced position. The act of pedalling means this balance point is quite wide, but you will find yourself pedalling increasingly quickly to maintain it. Once again, practice is needed to get used to the position. You should be able to pedal at a steady and constant rate, keeping your speed the same. How far can you wheelie?

Learning to wheelie is about bike balance and control. It is not used much on the track unless something else has gone wrong, but being able to extricate yourself from a difficult situation can be just as important as getting it right in the first place. One part of this technique that is used to great effect is the initial lift, which when used on a jump is called a pick-up. The idea is if you pick-up the front of a low jump, and place your front wheel over the top, you have effectively increased the size of the jump, and the benefit of the pump down its landing. This is an advanced technique, but it does highlight the importance of learning the basics in the correct way. You need to learn how to lift the bike using your pedal before you can learn to pick-up.

Stepping off the Back of the Bike from Stationary

To learn how to lift the front of the bike without using the pedal to assist, balance on your bike with it against a wall or similar obstacle. When you are ready, move suddenly forwards, then right back, until the wheel lifts. Do not pedal at all (the wall will stop you going anywhere anyway). Practise lifting the front wheel in this way until you can get it high enough to step off.

What happens here is, as you move slightly forwards, your bike moves back away from the wall. The effect is the same as what happens on the gate start. As you suddenly move back, the wheel then has the space to

start lifting. It will not move forwards if you are moving quickly enough – and you must be quick enough to surprise the bike.

Another thing that may happen as you move forwards is that the rear wheel will lift slightly. You can make it lift higher by allowing your legs to fold as you move forwards. This is called an endo, and is worth practising as it forms part of another BMX technique. Perhaps it is competition time again – who can endo the highest?

The Manual (Key Technique)

A manual involves rolling along with the front wheel raised. Usually you will raise the wheel with no pedal assistance – the shape of a track will help with this. Being able to lift a manual along the flat is possibly one of the hardest techniques to master, yet it is probably also one of the most important. It cannot be stressed enough that if you are able to balance and control a manual on the flat then you can manual any part of the track.

Manualling on flat.

Manualling through a jump.

Kids' race bikes are often relatively longer for the rider's size when compared to an adult on a full-size bike. This can mean that beginning a manual on the flat is much harder for them. An alternative to learning on the flat is to use a long, low tabletop. This allows the rider to get some assistance in lifting the wheel while still being required to learn their balance, keeping the wheel up along the top.

To manual you need to roll along at about jogging pace or a little faster. Ensure you are covering your brake. The rocking action is important, so move slightly forwards then 'surprise' the bike by immediately moving your weight back. The aim is to get the bike to lift purely by weight shift; this means that you will need to move further back than you think. Your final position will be lower than when doing the wheelie, and finding that exact point of balance will be that much harder.

The speed at which you are rolling will affect how quickly the bike lifts, and has a small effect on how far back you need to be to maintain the manual.

It is unlikely that you will master this quickly – do not underestimate how tough it is as a technique. A sharp jerk back on the handlebars may help younger riders. This does not pull the bike up, but simply adds an action that occurs naturally during the rocking action with bigger riders. The timing for this is critical, as it needs to occur just as the front of your bike is at its lightest – for a correctly sized bike, this will be when your arms are about to lock.

Once you have the front wheel up, you need to straighten your legs to be able to keep control. It should then be a little more comfortable. This straightening of the legs also provides the drive, and as you become more proficient by repeatedly compressing and extending your legs you can maintain your speed and manual for as long as necessary.

Manual a Double

Most riders start to manual on the track, probably over some doubles, before they learn to manual on the flat. It is generally easier – in fact the first time it is often accidental! Once you understand the correct technique, it can be adapted in a number of ways in order to manual efficiently on the track. Taking full advantage of the manual involves using many of the techniques in BMX.

When using a manual over a double, the shape of the track will help the front wheel lift. As you are getting this help, you will not need to move as far back. As the rear wheel passes over the lip of the take-off, push the bike down with your legs, extending them and raising your body. This provides a pump over the first part of the double. As you are crossing the double continue moving your body forwards and down into a folded state over the bike, so the front of the bike drops down. The front wheel needs to land just over the top on the landing.

On a large double, you push the bike over the jump by extending your arms and returning to the neutral position just as the rear wheel clears. At this point you can then implement the acceleration technique by moving your weight forwards and driving with the pedals.

On a low double, after the front wheel lands push with your arms the same way but keep your legs compressed, ready to use the pump technique as the rear wheel clears the top.

The Pick-up

A pick-up involves lifting the front wheel on to or over an obstacle, and is done to maintain speed, keeping the bike in the direction of travel with the least resistance. It is mostly used over smaller obstacles. The size of such obstacles means that, when taking them at high speeds, there is not enough time to react to the bike. The technique is most commonly used over a roller, and these are often placed at the bottom of the start hill. The pick-up effectively increases the size of the obstacle, allowing you to make it smoother.

Picking-up over a roller/speed bump.

Picking-up and manualling through a jump.

There are two types of pick-up. If your intention is to lift the front wheel and keep pedalling, the pedal action is used to assist the lift. The force of the pedal to lift the bike completely (which would be used with the wheelie) cannot be used, as the rider is already pedalling as hard as he or she can. Instead, you lift as you would a manual on the flat, but time it so that the lift corresponds with a pedal just passing over the top of its path. You will not need to lean back quite as far. Keep pedalling and allow the back wheel to follow. This is mostly used on single rollers and low step-ups.

If you do not want to pedal, lift the front wheel just as you would a manual. Sometimes you may want to place the wheel down on the jump, and occasionally you may want to maintain the manual as the rear wheel rides up the jump. This type of pick-up is usual on rhythm sections, or at the start of a combination jump.

Advanced Manuals

Once you are able to manual on the flat, and are able to use your legs to drive the bike, you can combine this with the pumping technique. The result is the ability to manual an entire straight, pumping the rear wheel while maintaining the front-wheel lift. Do not expect to be doing this in a few months, or even years. Reaching this level of ability will take most riders hundreds of hours of practice and involve a combination of most of the techniques in BMX.

SIZES

Smaller bikes often have shorter cranks so pedalling over a jump is easier.

Leaving the Ground – All Wheels Together

The 'Pop'

It is probably clear by now that each new technique is simply a combination of the same movements. The last of those movements is the pop. Again, it is not entirely new, and is simply the action of extending from the folded position. To make it a pop, it has to be done in a very sudden and explosive manner, and without pushing too hard on the pedals. It is almost as if you are attempting to jump off the bike, but your sudden action 'surprises' your bike and, as you rise, so will it.

The Bunny Hop (Key Technique)

In the bunny hop, both wheels are lifted from the ground. There are two main versions: one where you lift your front wheel followed by your back wheel, and the other where you lift both wheels at once. Both are important.

Lifting both wheels at once from the flat is very simple. Roll along at about walking speed, then suddenly and explosively 'drop' and 'pop'. The drop is a full fold, bending arms and legs and getting as low as possible on the bike. It is very important to keep neutral, staying over the saddle and not moving forwards or backwards. Your pedals should remain level – but this will be second nature to you by now.

After a bit of practice, you should be leaving the ground, but not very high. To gain height you need to add another movement, so that the bunny hop becomes 'drop', 'pop' and 'fold'. The final fold is again just bending your arms and legs and allowing the bike to keep rising, even though you may have stopped. As the bike starts to fall, remember to extend again, then fold again as it lands.

Bunny-hopping over a funbox.

Folding again is also called 'absorbing', the aim of which is to 'soften' the impact of you and your bike on the ground. As the bike lands and suddenly stops falling, you continue moving by folding and stop yourself much more gently.

So the bunny hop can be broken down into the following series of movements: drop, pop, fold, extend, absorb. None of these are new movements, but this combination is a more advanced technique and the way in which the movements are carried out becomes much more important.

The other style of bunny hop requires you to lift your front wheel first, as is usually learned at a slightly faster speed. First manual, then drop and pop only with your legs. Fold with your legs, but also push forwards on your handlebars. This will 'roll' the rear of the bike up and straighten it and allow you to land in the same way as with the first bunny hop. Greater height can usually be achieved using this method. As you become better at this, practise the bunny hop without straightening your bike, land on your back wheel and retain the manual.

Controlling the Bike in the Air

You do have some control over your bike while it is in the air. The main decision you need to make is whether you want to land with both wheels together, rear wheel first

---

> **BUNNY HOP TECHNIQUE TIPS**
>
> When practising your bunny hops on the flat, great care must be taken if landing front wheel first. Do not have your weight too far forwards and return to neutral as quickly as you can as your wheel lands.

---

or front wheel first. You also need to decide which is the best way to achieve the desired result:

- Both wheels together – keep your weight central, extend arms and legs equally.
- Front wheel first – move your weight over the front of the bike, or extend your arms more than your legs.
- Rear wheel first – move your weight over the back of the bike, or extend your legs more than your arms.

Practising all these different landings becomes very important when moving on to the final technique – jumping.

Jumping

Jumping is what BMX racing is all about. It is used to 'smooth' the shape of the track and allow the rider to shorten the distance they need to travel. The great thing about jumping is that nothing new needs to be taught – everything you need you have already learned.

It is important to consider speed. When riders first begin jumping they rely mostly on speed rather than technique. Speed is important, but using speed to compensate for poor technique is not the answer. The speed at which you approach the obstacle determines the maximum distance you can possibly travel, but how much of that maximum distance you

---

> **SKILL LIST**
>
> As techniques start to encompass more and more movements, it is usually a good idea to break them down into a series of simpler descriptions, so that a rider can more easily remember them. For a full list of those that are currently used, along with descriptions, see page 131.

Jumping over a funbox.

can travel is down to your technique. It is very easy to jump a small jump simply by riding over it as fast as you can, but having control over your height and distance and achieving a controlled and smooth landing is all down to technique.

The jump technique may be broken up into a series of required movements:

- As the bike rolls up the landing, you will *fold* to allow the bike to rise.
- As the front wheel passes over the top, you will *pop* to let the bike keep rising.
- As the bike leaves the ground, you will *fold* to gain the necessary height.
- As the bike arcs over the jump, you will *extend*, arms first, to roll the bike over into the optimum landing. Your aim is to get the front wheel to land just over the top of the landing, with the rear wheel following. You may need to move your weight forwards to help with this.
- As the bike lands you will *absorb* the impact by folding.
- Once the back wheel is on the ground, you will *extend* to push the bike down the

landing and gain as much speed as you can – pumping. If you have moved over the front of the bike, at this stage you need to be moving back to neutral.

This can be shortened so that it is easier to remember: fold, pop, fold, push (arms), absorb, push.

Practising jumping on the track can be a problem, as not only do you have to consider the jump itself, but also getting past the obstacles correctly before the jump and after the jump. A few tracks have 'training sections', with a small tabletop built with lots of space before and after. While there are not many at the moment, as more BMX qualified coaches get involved with club operations and tracks, there should be more. A tabletop is usually the most forgiving style of jump on which to practise jumping. Some clubs will use a board to 'fill in' a double to make it more forgiving when riders are learning this technique.

You can also practise your jumping by using portable ramps or visiting your local skatepark and using the funbox.

The path of a rider jumping a jump.

Terms and Techniques Described

From the basic list of movements, and full information on applying these to the techniques, coaches can begin to introduce shorter descriptions. Every technique on the bike can be broken down into a series of movements, or 'actions' as the current coaching theory books like to call them.

The basic terms used include the following:

- pedalling;
- rolling;
- neutral (staying central on the bike);
- balancing (being balanced on the bike, left/right and forwards/backwards);
- reacting (reacting to something, usually the start sequence);
- leaning (sideways usually with the bike. Pedals will be level or outside pedal down);
- forwards (moving your weight forwards);
- backwards (moving your weight backwards);
- folding (bending arms and legs while the bike is rising so that you are closer to the bike);

- absorbing (bending in reaction to the bike suddenly stopping on landing);
- dropping (bending so you are lower on the bike);
- extending (extending arms and legs);
- pushing (pushing the bike away from you);
- popping (jumping up away from the bike).

These terms can be used to describe any technique in BMX, for example:

- **Gate start:** balance – react – forwards – pedal – neutral – pedal.
- **Manual (from rolling):** neutral – roll – back – balance – roll.
- **Pumping:** roll – fold – push (arms then legs) – roll.

As you become more proficient as a rider, combining these 'actions' becomes smoother, as you learn to move seamlessly and effortlessly from one to the next. Eventually you will forget the different, separate actions you combine to jump – you will just jump. At this point, you will be unconsciously competent. Remember to keep practising to maintain (at the very least) or improve your technique.

Remember this is not a self-teach book. This advice has been designed to help you find a good coach, and to help you understand what that coach is teaching you. He or she will almost certainly describe things slightly differently. Coaches should always be developing their skills and techniques, attending courses and workshops, observing and being observed by other coaches, sharing ideas with other coaches and reading a few books, and as a result of this they will have updated their methods, found better descriptions, added new ideas and absorbed a whole host of other information.

A rider learning how to jump using ramps.

CHAPTER 8

GETTING INVOLVED

Now you know practically everything there is to know about BMX racing, you will no doubt want to get started. There are many different ways to get involved. First, the best thing to do is to ride. There are over forty different clubs based in the seven regions across the UK. All of them will be open to new members, and there is no fee for watching a practice session or club race. To find your nearest club either consult the British Cycling website or the list below.

Clubs

South, SouthBMX.co.uk

Andover, andoverbmx.co.uk
Barking and Dagenham, badbmx.com
Bournemouth, bournemouthbmx.co.uk
Brixton, brixtonbmxclub.com
East Kent, eastkentbmx.co.uk
Gosport, gosportbmx.co.uk
Hayes Hawks, hawksbmx.co.uk
Hersden, hersdenbmx.co.uk
Peckham, peckhambm.co.uk

South West

Bath, bathbmx.com
Bideford, bidefordbombersbmx.co.uk
Bristol, bristolbmxclub.com
Burnham-on-Sea, burnhambmx.com
Cornwall, cornwallbmx.co.uk
Decoy, decoy-bmx.co.uk
Duchy, duchypirates.co.uk
Exeter, exeter-eagles.co.uk

Forest of Dean,
  geocities.com/forestofdeanbmx
Tredegar, tredbmx.wordpress.com

East Anglia, BMXEast.com

Braintree, braintreebmx.co.uk
Ipswich, ipswichbmx.co.uk
Milton Keynes, mkbmx.com
Norwich, norwichbmx.co.uk
Peterborough,
  peterboroughphantomsbmx.co.uk
Royston, roystonrockets.co.uk

Midlands, MidlandsRegionalBMX.co.uk

Bulwell, nottinghamoutlaws.com
Chesterfield, chesterfieldbmx.co.uk
Derby, cyclederby.co.uk
Doncaster, dbmx.co.uk
Mansfield, mansfieldbmx.co.uk
Redditch Premiers,
  redditchpremiers.co.uk
Rotherham, rotherhambmx.com
Stockingford Crusaders,
  stockingfordcrusaders.webeden.com

North, NorthRegionBMX.co.uk

Bradford, bradfordbmxbandits.org.uk
Crewe, cheshireghostriders.blogspot.com
Hartlepool, northeastbmx.com
Leeds, leedsbmx.co.uk
Lytham Goldcoast,
  goldcoastbmxclub.co.uk
Manchester, manchesterbmx.co.uk
Mid Lancs, midlancsbmx.co.uk
Preston, prestonpiratesbmxclub.com

Isle of Man
Ramsey BMX Club,
  ramseybmx.blogspot.com

Scotland
Ride BMX Racing Club,
  Cumbernauld, ridebmxracing.com
Titans BMX Glasgow, titansbmx.co.uk

Volunteers

BMX racing is not just about riding BMX. While it might seem like it is just one person (or eight, in a race) riding a bike around a track, it takes a whole team of people to make it happen. Event organizers, track officials and first aiders are all needed to help an event run smoothly. Without volunteers, BMX racing as a sport would not be possible.

Due to the low-budget ethos of BMX racing, the sport relies heavily upon volunteers to help its riders and spectators. Parents are actively encouraged to lend a hand where and when they can, as this makes it far more enjoyable for everyone involved.

There are a wide range of jobs that need doing in BMX racing, which will all need to be undertaken by at least one person. The more people who volunteer their help, the better the club runs and the better the sport becomes.

First Aiders
BMX racing is an extreme sport with an element of danger. First aiders are often needed to help riders who crash during a race or practice session. Without people capable of offering first aid to fallen riders, races would not be possible. While the majority of crashes

A first aider watching the racing.

in BMX result in nothing more than scrapes, bruises and a drop in confidence, there is always the possibility of more substantial injuries such as sprains or broken bones. Clearly, having an appropriate number of first aiders always helps a club.

Gate Controllers

One of the main jobs in BMX racing is dropping the gate. It is the job of the gate controller to operate the gate in a safe manner, ensuring that no riders ride over the gate when it is about to come up. They must let all the riders know when the gate is about to come up, and when it is about to drop, and make sure that all riders stick to the rules set out by the club. Controlling the gate provides a great opportunity to interact with the riders, as there will always be some people waiting near the gate.

Marshals

BMX tracks are constantly changing in elevation and direction, meaning that, if a rider

Gate calling and controlling can be a fun job.

A marshal indicates that a rider has fallen.

crashes; the gate controller might not be able to see them. This is why BMX racing has marshals standing on top of berms, watching the race. If a rider falls and fails to get back up straight away, the marshal will hold up a flag indicating that there is a rider down and the gate should not be dropped for the next batch of riders. This makes it safer for both the riders and the first aiders, as it ensures that no races are run while there is still an injured rider on the track. Once the rider has cleared the track, the marshal will drop the flag, indicating that it is safe to run the next race.

Commentators

Commentators are needed for all levels of racing, as their commentary is sometimes the only way the spectators will hear about the race. Knowing the riders' names, plates and any other information always makes the commentary more fun and interesting to listen to, and a good commentator will usually have been part of BMX for quite some time. Commentary jobs at the very top of the sport are paid, but most are not. This does not detract from the fun, and most commentators offer their services just for the thrill.

Finish-Line Ladies

Mainly referred to as 'finish-line ladies' (because most of them are mums of riders at the event), these volunteers are positioned on the finish line and charged with the job of noting who finishes in which position. It requires a fast eye and an even faster hand. They write down the number plates of the riders in the order in which they finish, and confer after to ensure that they have all recorded the same results. Although it might seem like a small task, these people are responsible for making sure that everyone receives the correct points and places – an integral part of BMX racing.

At higher-level competitions (Nationals upwards), finish-line technology will be used. This can decide to the millimetre which riders have finished in which position. Some races have been won and lost by a tyre's width, and this is when finish-line technology comes into its own.

Commissaries/Referees

As with any sport, BMX needs referees. Although the vast majority of riders stick to the rules and have no disagreements (at the lower levels, anyway), referees are required to watch out for a number of issues:

- crossing white lines/cutting the corners;
- overly aggressive overtaking manoeuvres;
- bad language;
- illegal clothing (see Chapter 2);
- illegal equipment (see Chapter 3);
- safeguarding of children;
- riders breaking the rules in any other way;
- any other issues regarding racing.

In order to be a BMX racing referee, an individual will have to go on several different courses and pass a number of tests or exams. This makes sure that only those who have proven themselves proficient are allowed to referee a race.

There are several different levels of referee within cycling, starting at Assistant Commissary, moving up to Regional Commissary and National Commissary, and then to the highest level, the UCI Commissary.

Photographers

All riders like to see photos of themselves riding. Not only does it help them to see how they are riding (track position, technique, stance, and so on), but it can also make them look good. While there may be a large number of photographers in regular attendance at National races, there are very few photographers at club level. Both riders and clubs are always appreciative of any photography anyone can do for them and, as they will (usually) be happy for a photographer to sell their photos to the riders, it is a win-win situation. Rather than just turning up at a track unannounced (unless you are known there), it is always best to ask a club official if it is OK for you to take some photos. They may ask you to sign a statement regarding child safety and anonymity, but most clubs will be more than happy to have photos taken.

Videographers

Videographers at BMX events are even rarer than photographers – it is much more difficult to film a race than to photograph it. While most people have a digital camera handy, not all will have a camera capable of videoing the high-speed action and the necessary software to edit clips together. However, a film recording can be a valuable training tool, much like a photograph, allowing riders to analyse their riding style. It can help riders to break down how they jump, manual and pump their way around a track. Both videos and photographs are used extensively in the training process, both before and after a race. It can be very

helpful for a rider to get some track knowledge before they go to an event and videos also allow those who did not attend the event to get an overview of the proceedings.

As with photographers, a club will generally be happy to have a person videoing the session, as long as they ask the event organizers first.

Writers

BMX clubs take a lot of running, and this leaves very little time for activities such as producing race reports. Sometimes a club will have a volunteer who writes up the news on how its riders have fared at various events. Having a person write for a club can help the club to have more of an active membership. If a club has a regularly updated website or literature, the current members will enjoy it more and new members will be encouraged to join.

Website Designers/Webmasters/ Graphic Designers

Not everyone is proficient at creating, updating and maintaining websites, yet almost everyone has a computer and Internet access.

Potential volunteers talk to a club official.

Club officials helping riders.

This is why making sure a club has an active website helps it to grow in popularity and presence, as people will be more likely to come down to the track and ride if they can find up-to-date information online. Although most clubs do have a website of some description, it is always best to enquire if they need any help if you have the expertise.

Depending on the club and its activities, it may need a designer for anything from club logos, race shirts and club gear, to leaflets advertising the club.

Gate Callers

At race events it is important for everyone to be in the correct gates at the correct times. This ensures that the event runs smoothly and quickly, with no mistakes. To make sure this happens, the event will need someone to stand at the top of the start hill and call out the names of the riders in the next race, as well as the number of the gate from which they are starting. This not only helps the riders to get into the correct lane, but also helps the commentator to say the right names and the event organizers to get the day's racing done as smoothly as possible. Every race will need a gate caller, and club races particularly are in need of volunteers.

Money Handlers

At every session the club runs, there will be a need for someone to take the money from the riders when they come to pay for gates or racing. Making sure everyone has paid their fees, and that all the riders have been marked as either attending or not attending, is a very important part of running the club.

Coaches

Riders will always benefit from training delivered by an officially endorsed coach – someone trained by British Cycling. While there are many coaches at the top of the sport coaching potential Olympic athletes and professional BMX racers, there is a significant lack of coaches training riders at club level. This can be for a number of reasons – lack of training, lack of motivation, costs, location. Coaching children and adults to ride faster and more confidently can be a very rewarding experience, however, and one to look out for should the opportunity arise.

Results Handlers

Once the races have been run and the finish-line ladies have discussed and verified their results, the information is handed over to a results handler, who will then generate the finals sheets and points. This can be done either on paper (on specifically made 'moto sheets') or on a computer. They will usually be in charge of generating the moto sheets, finals sheets and points for the race. Making sure everyone is in the correct race and is given the correct points is a complex task, and one that is usually done by someone who has been trained in doing so.

Track Maintenance

Most BMX tracks are outdoors, and as such the weather can take its toll on them. This leads to regular track maintenance being necessary, especially before a race. Repairing ruts, adding dirt and sweeping the track all need to be done from time to time, and clubs will usually ask for help from volunteers when planning to repair the track in any way.

Team Managers

When a team is sponsored by a large company (such as Freeagent or GT), there will usually be a number of riders all riding on the same

A coach talks to riders.

bike and with the same kit. A team manager is responsible for ensuring that all of these riders are encouraged and motivated, and know what is expected of them, in terms of both results and behaviour, identifies areas where riders can improve and handles any other issues the team may have.

While most of these jobs will be unpaid, they all need doing, and any club for which you volunteer will be very grateful. BMX is a very family-oriented sport, with parents and children being able to compete in the same events. It does need volunteers to help push it forwards and, at the lower end of the sport, to keep it going. Although some of the jobs

may already be filled at your local track – a club with a thriving member base will probably have more volunteers, whereas a smaller club will require more help – no club will turn away a willing volunteer, and most will actively search for something for you to do. Helping your local track can be fun and rewarding, and something that almost everyone in the BMX community – rider, spectator, parent or otherwise – will have done at some point. It is a great way to give something back to the club.

So, there is more than one way to get involved in BMX racing. Whether you are riding or not, you will find something for everyone in the family to enjoy.

Sponsor marquees line the side of a track.

FURTHER INFORMATION

There are a number of useful websites and publications that will help you in discovering BMX racing, buying equipment and finding out regular BMX news.

BMX Information

British Cycling
The official governing body for almost all cycling events in the UK. The website contains rankings, current points standings, cycling photos and videos, as well as information regarding racing licences.

British Cycling, Stuart Street, Manchester
  M11 4DQ
Tel 0161 274 2000
Fax 0161 274 2001
info@britishcycling.org.uk
britishcycling.org.uk

BMX Mania
An American-owned BMX racing news website run by BMX photographer Jerry Landrum, which features news on BMX racing from across the globe, along with photos of races and product information.

bmxmania.com

BMX Talk
British BMX racing forum. A great place to ask for advice on practically anything BMX-related. It also has a 'For Sale' section, where riders can buy and sell equipment.

bmxtalk.com

UCI
The official event runner for all high-level BMX races, its website has useful information, as well as events, rankings, photos and videos.

uci.ch

FAT BMX
US BMX racing news website, with all the information on the American BMX series, as well as information on products and anything else interesting in the world of BMX racing.

fatbmx.com

BMX Publications

Twenty24 (2024)
Europe's premier BMX racing magazine, *2024* covers racing from across the globe, as well as featuring product reviews, local round-ups, columns from famous riders and anything else related to BMX racing. *Twenty24* is at every National race selling the magazine, and has a team of highly skilled photographers and writers covering BMX events from every perspective.

twenty24bmx.com

Pro BMX Skills
Available from the USA, a BMX training book aimed at those with a lot of racing experience, and endorsed by US Olympic team coach Greg Romero ('Coach G'). Its training methods should be considered only by experienced riders who have already conferred with a coach.

probmxskills.com

INDEX

RELATED TITLES FROM CROWOOD

Cycle Road Racing

Tom Newman

ISBN 978 1 84797 434 1

128pp,
120 illustrations

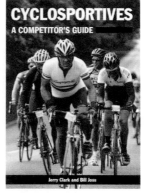

Cyclosportives A Competitor's Guide

Jerry Clark and Steve Joss

ISBN 978 1 84797 244 6

144pp,
160 illustrations

Mountain Biking Crowood Sports Guide

James McKnight

ISBN 978 1 84797 419 8

112pp,
200 illustrations

Triathlon Crowood Sports Guide

Steve Trew

ISBN 978 1 84797 170 8

96pp,
100 illustrations

In case of difficulty in ordering, contact the Sales Office:

The Crowood Press Ltd
Ramsbury   Wiltshire   SN8 2HR

Tel: 44 (0) 1672 520320
enquiries@crowood.com
www.crowood.com